THE EVERYTHING KIDS'® BUGS BOOK

Puzzles, games, and trivia for hours of squishy fun

Kathi Wagner

Adams Media Corporation
Avon, Massachusetts

Published by Adams Media Corporation
57 Littlefield Street, Avon, MA 02322. U.S.A.
www.adamsmedia.com

ISBN: 1-58062-892-3

Printed in the United States of America.

J I H G F E D C B A

Library of Congress Cataloging-in-Publication Data
Wagner, Kathi.
The everything kids' bugs book / Kathi Wagner.
p. cm. (An everything series book)
Summary: Explores the world of insects--where to find them, how to attract them, how to help them grow--and the characteristics of specific kinds of bugs from around the world. Includes related activities and word lists.
ISBN 1-58062-892-3
1. Insects--Juvenile literature. [1. Insects.] I. Title. II. Series.
Everything series.
QL467.2 .W335 2003
595.7--dc21 2002152404

Cover illustrations by Dana Regan.
Interior illustrations by Kurt Dolber and Barry Littmann.
Puzzles by Beth Blair.

Puzzle Power Software by Centron Software Technologies, Inc. was used to create puzzle grids.

Contents

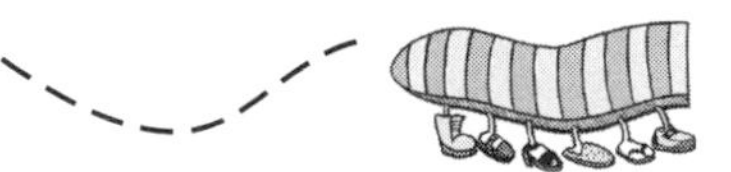

Contents

Introduction

Welcome to the World of Bugs!

Are you into creepy, crawly, slimy, squirmy, squishy, squashy fun? Well, this is the book for you! Bugs, as you know, are everywhere—in the air, in the water, in the earth, and all around you. Hundreds of thousands of these creatures have been discovered over the years and even more are found each year! In *The Everything® Kids' Bugs Book*, you will find everything you need to become an expert bug catcher, and perhaps even to make the next bug discovery! Did you know that if you discover a new kind of bug, you get to name it?

So, how can you begin your bug hunt? First off, you need to know where to look for them. Luckily, this book will guide you into the hidden world of bugs. You'll learn where to find them and how to attract them—even how to help them grow. Insects have been frightening and fascinating us for millions of years, and it's no wonder—what other animals can smell with their antennas, taste with their feet, or hear with their hair? Not to mention all that stinging, screaming, and oozing. And now, you have the chance to explore all the mysteries of bugs for yourself.

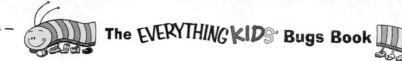

But there is so much more! With the help of this book, you can be the ringmaster of your own flea circus, the crew chief of a bug racing team, and the Olympic coach of bug gymnastics. You can also be a night watchman, a safari hunter, a pirate, and a magician. And that's just the beginning! See if you can earn your black belt in bug self-defense by learning the fine arts of spitting, hissing, screaming, and making others scream too. And if you're really into adventure, you can visit the "tombs" and eat a few bugs, before they eat you!

You will have to rely on your skills as a marksman as you shoot and spot your own T-shirt with a tie-dye squirt gun, and on your construction skills as a foreman and cardboard engineer. Before you are through with this book, you will also have the chance to be a detective, a weather forecaster, and a travel guide. So, gather your gear, get out your old shoes, round up your friends, and warn your family—you're about to have some serious fun! Here we go!

Chapter 1

Catch Me If You Can!

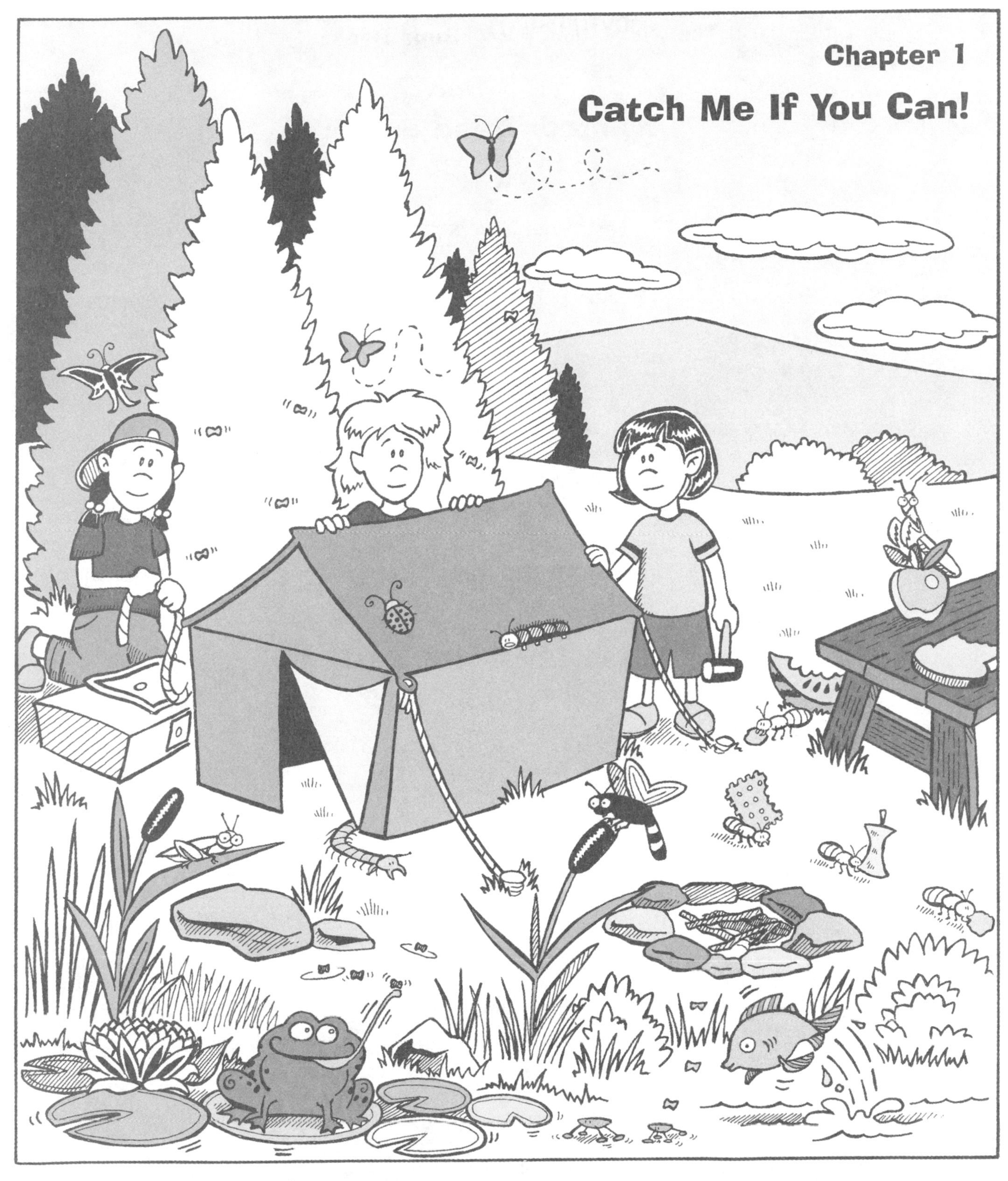

Wanted: Dead or Alive

Collecting bugs can be a fun activity. And it's more fun if you catch your bugs alive. Why? There are two reasons for this. One, you can learn a lot about an insect's behavior by watching it "in action." And two, you need to keep in mind that bugs are living creatures and deserve good treatment. You need to be humane and show some mercy to your new friends. You can catch your bugs, watch and study them, feed and water them . . . and when you're through, let them go!

However, if you find bugs that are already dead, they won't mind if you add them to your permanent collection. A bug's life is very short compared to ours; many die in a day or two after becoming an adult insect. If you look for those that have already died, you'll be sure to find quite a few. Pinning them to Styrofoam and keeping them in a box is a great way to start your collection.

WORDS to KNOW

humane: To be *humane* means to treat other people and other living creatures with mercy and compassion. The word *humane* comes from "human," because kind behavior is what makes us human. Remember that when you go out on your next bug hunt!

Oh No! Not the Net!

You don't have to go out and buy a lot of things to be a bug hunter. Many of the items you will need can be found around the house. For instance, you can make a net for catching bugs with a wire coat hanger: just bend the wire into a circle, tape it to a stick, and staple or sew a fine mesh cloth to the wire.

The rest of your bug hunting kit may include the following tools:

- A few **small boxes** (like film canisters or butter tubs) where you can keep the bugs you find—don't

forget to make small holes so that your bugs can breathe
- A **magnifying glass** for searching for the littlest critters
- A **small net** to catch water insects
- A **camera** (if you want to "catch them on film")
- A small **hand shovel** for digging
- **Food** for the insects and for you
- A **bag** to carry all your tools and supplies

Now that you have the tools, do you have the talent? Some people take bug collecting very seriously. For some, catching and studying bugs is a career. These people are called *entomologists*. It's one of the many jobs you could have working with bugs. Some of the other careers that could really "bug" you are:

- **Exterminators:** People who help you get rid of bugs.
- **Crop scouts:** Workers who check for insects in and around crops.
- **Honey farmers:** Farmers who specialize in raising bees and collecting their honey.
- **Disease specialists:** Researchers who look for causes and cures of diseases caused or spread by insects.
- **Forest rangers:** People who take care of forests; one of their duties is to protect trees from the bugs that may harm them.
- **Crop dusters:** People who fly planes to dust crops with insecticides in order to protect them from being eaten by bugs.
- **Environmentalists:** Those who keep an eye on the world and the things that affect our surroundings.

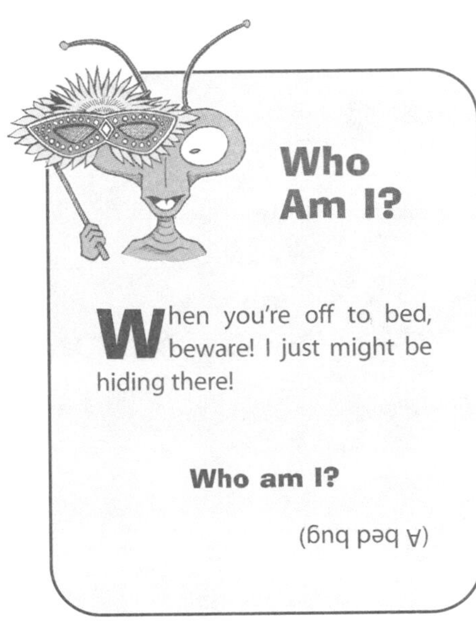

Who Am I?

When you're off to bed, beware! I just might be hiding there!

Who am I?

(A bed bug) *(printed upside down)*

entomologist: A scientist who studies the world and behaviors of insects and classifies them into groups.

insecticide: A substance created to kill insects or insect pests. Insecticides come in small containers for home use or can be applied by professional exterminators.

Set a Bug Trap

It's time to set the trap and see what you catch! All you need is a sheet that you can spread under a tree or bush. As you lightly tap the branches, a few bugs are sure to come flying down onto the sheet. Once they have landed, collect the ones you want and place them in your bug containers.

Now, you can set up an entire zoo full of bugs! In fact, you can set up an aquarium to represent the outdoor environment where you found your bugs. To make your bugs comfortable, you might need to add the following into the aquarium:

- **grass**
- **water**
- **leaves and twigs**
- **rocks**
- **food**
- **soil**
- **shade**
- **air**

Then, you can release your bugs into their new environment and see what happens.

Beware of the Praying Mantis

It may just happen that among all the bugs you catch, you'll find a praying mantis. In this case, beware! These vicious bugs will eat anyone they meet on their way, so keep your other bugs away from them. And keep your hands away too—these bugs do bite.

You'll know a praying mantis when you see one. This long slender insect spends most of its time watching what everyone around it is doing with its big green eyes. The reason it's called a *praying* mantis is because of the way it holds its front legs together, as if in prayer. Actually, what the mantis is doing is watching and waiting for a meal (another insect) to walk by.

Praying mantises like to dwell in bushes and small trees, but you can also find them almost any place where there are lots of bugs around—in flower or vegetable gardens and even on potted plants. If your yard doesn't have any praying mantises, you may want to buy an egg case in the spring (through a nursery catalog or over the Internet) and raise your own mantises outside.

If you look closely at the eye of a praying mantis, you will see that it has a pupil very similar to a human eye. A mantis is one of the few insects that is able to move its head all around to look at things. Another thing you may want to watch for is the mantis cleaning its feelers with its jaws. Sometimes they act more like a cat than an insect.

Keep the Peace!

When you are out to catch different kinds of bugs, be sure that you have a separate jar for each kind. You never know what will happen if you put moths and caterpillars, or beetles and butterflies, or other combinations together. These bugs may not get along with each other!

Hunting in the Dark

If you're after live bugs, one of the best times to catch them is after dark. If you look and listen outside your door for a few minutes, you'll discover a whole other world out there.

A prepared hunter always brings supplies. For your nighttime hunting kit you may want:

- 1 or 2 **plastic jars** with lids (you can poke holes in these before hunting)
- **Grass** to place in the jar
- A **white sheet** or cloth
- A **net**
- A **cardboard box**
- A **flashlight**
- A spade or **hand shovel**

What would you get if you crossed a parrot and a bumblebee?

A bird that talks all the time about how busy it is.

FUN FACT

Dizzying Acrobatics

If you watch a moth flying toward a light, you will notice that it spirals or circles until it reaches the light. The moth will turn in the direction of the light that is shining the brightest toward its closest eye. Depending on which direction the moth comes upon the light, it may spiral left or right.

Going on a hunt for fireflies or glowworms is best undertaken during the months of June, July, and August. The darker it is outside, the easier it is to see them. You can use a net to catch the fireflies—if you're really quick, you can even catch them with your hands. The glowworms will glow from underneath the ground, because they are actually in the earth. Capturing a glowworm requires a small amount of digging and sifting. Once you have your glowing friends, you can place them in the jar.

Many nighttime dwellers are drawn to light; in fact, did you know that one way to tell a moth from a butterfly is that moths fly toward the light? That's because moths are nighttime creatures and butterflies only appear during the day. If you want to see a few moths up close and personal, you can attract them by draping a sheet near an outside light or by laying it over your flashlight. When they come and sit down on the cloth, you can trap them with your net and put them in the jar.

The New Bug in Town

Dr. Pheromone has discovered a new kind of moth. Use the clues below to figure out which of the moths pictured is the new one!

1. The new moth is in a column that has two beetles.
2. The new moth is in a row that has two other moths.
3. There is no moth directly to the right of the new moth.

HINT: Columns go up and down, and rows go side to side.

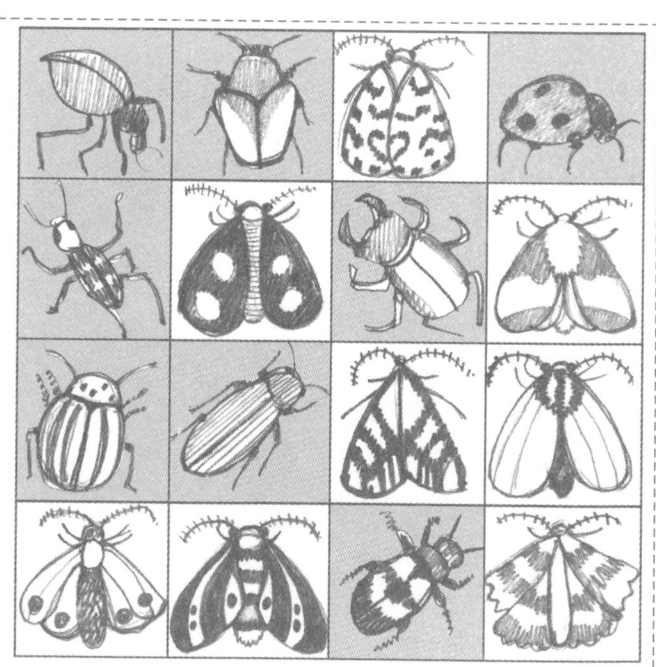

Let's Play "Clue"

Now that you have your flashlight out, you might as well have some fun with it. Why not set up a clue hunt? Get some plastic bugs, or draw them on paper, and spread them out throughout your backyard or another area that's safe for kids to play. (Using glow-in-the-dark objects such as paints and stickers will make this even more fun!) Then, make a list of clues, like these:

I don't live in the ground, or up in a tree—
Somewhere that is wet is where you'll find me.

(Water bug)

When it's late at night,
I circle toward the light.

(Moth)

Ladybug, ladybug, fly away home,
We're tired of you eating us. Please leave us alone.

(Flowers)

I spend most of my day hanging upside down,
And I land on your food when you're not around.

(A fly)

Now, can you think of some of your own clues?

What has six legs, wings, sucks blood, and eats cheese?

A mouse-quito!

Who Am I?

I have eyes that are small and set far apart. Up close my head sort of looks a like the head of a whale. But unlike the whale, I prefer fire to water. You can find me spending most of my time by your furnace or boiler. To some people I am considered a pest or a brat. **Who am I?**

(A firebrat)

Make Your Own Flashing Bug

If you want to make your own flashing bug, here's what you do. Make a bug out of cardboard—this is your chance to be creative, so use your imagination. You can make it as big and as complicated as you want to. To make a flash for your bug, you need to take apart an old battery-operated flashlight. First, try to see how the flashlight works. Can you see how the electricity runs from the battery to the light bulb? Save these two parts, and also get two copper wires (your parents might have some in their toolbox; if not, you can purchase them from a hardware or home-improvement store), tape, and some foam.

When you've got everything ready, take a copper wire and tape one end to the metallic end of the light bulb and the other end to the top of the battery. Connect the other wire between the same place on the light bulb and to the other end of the battery. When the connection is right, the bulb should turn on; if you break the connection, the light will shut off.

You can produce flashing by taping a small piece of foam between the copper wire and the battery. This will keep the wire close to the battery without it touching, so to make the flashes, all you need to do is press down on the foam, allowing the wire to touch the battery. Then, tape the cardboard body of the bug to the battery, with the light bulb barely showing out the end of the bug. Now all you have to do is press down on the foam spot and your bug will flash.

FUN FACT

A Flash of Love

Fireflies flash a signal to communicate with their potential mates. If you notice some fireflies flash differently than others, it's because there are many varieties of fireflies and each one has a different timing to their "flash."

Two flies are in the kitchen. How can you tell which one is the football player?

Easy—it's the one in the Sugar Bowl!

▶ Try This

Powered by Bugs

You can make a lightning-bug lantern: All you need is a jar with a lid and some lightening bugs. Do you think that the lantern will work best with more lightning bugs? Keep adding them in, and see if the light gets brighter.

Word Caterpillar

Fill this hungry caterpillar with letters! Write the answer to each numbered clue into the caterpillar, placing one letter in each section. The last letter of one word is the first letter of the next. To answer the riddle, copy the letters in the shaded sections onto the dotted lines.

HINT: Write the answers in order from the head of the caterpillar to its tail, even if it looks like you're spelling backward!

1. A series of names, numbers, or other things.
2. One of the five senses.
3. Body part used for hearing.
4. Spring bird with a red breast.
5. A crazy or silly person.
6. A game where someone is "it."

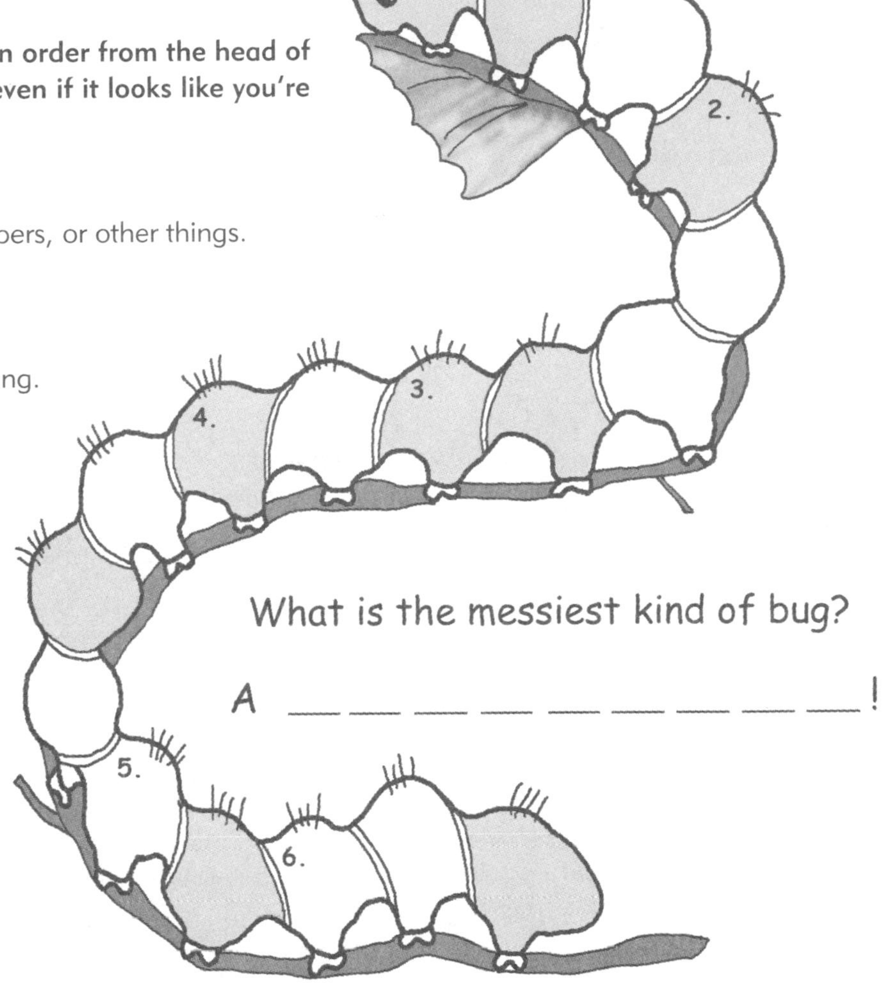
1.
2.
3.
4.
5.
6.
What is the messiest kind of bug?
A ___ ___ ___ ___ ___ ___ ___ ___ ___!

Bug-Eyed Adventures

Now that you've had a chance to catch and examine quite a few bugs, what do you think? Different, huh? One thing in particular that strikes many people is the structure of bug eyes. Compared to its body, an insect's eyes are much larger in scale. One reason for this is their eyes are compound, which means they have multiple eyes combined in one. Some bugs have less than 10 (six-sided) lenses in their compound eyes, while others have up to 30,000. All of these lenses work together to form the picture the insect sees: the greater the number of lenses, the sharper the vision. To experience what some believe is an example of how a bug sees, try looking through a prism (a many-sided smooth piece of glass). Many prisms are used for sun catchers, because they send the sun's rays shooting in all directions when sunlight shines through it.

When the sun shines through a multifaceted object like a bug's eye, a prism, or a glass of water, its rays will bend and cause the light to change. You can try creating your own prism by using several clear glass marbles that you put in a glass jar. What happens when you set the jars on a sunny windowsill? What happens when you add water to the marbles?

FUN FACT

Powerful Vision

Because of the way their honeycomb-shaped lenses work, insects see many images at the same time. And, they are able to see in ultraviolet colors. Ultraviolet vision is very similar to what we see when we turn on a black light. It is also a lot like the view through night-vision goggles, which explains how bugs can see so well in the dark.

▶ Try This

Solar Paper for Stellar Art

Let your imagination loose with some solar photographic paper (see if your parents can buy it at the local photography shop). When you expose this special paper to direct sunlight, the shadows over the paper remain permanent. For instance, if you place a butterfly on the paper and then put it in the sun, the paper will retain the silhouette of the butterfly.

It's Like a Kaleidoscope

Another way to experience compound vision is with a kaleidoscope. Making one yourself is fairly easy too! You will need only six things:

- A **cardboard roll** (the kind in the center of a toilet paper roll)
- 2 clear, round, stacking **bead containers or sorters** that screw together. (These are available at most large hobby stores.)
- **Several beads** in different colors
- Three pieces of **thin cardboard** cut into rectangles that are 4 inches long and 1½ inches wide
- **Adhesive tape**
- **Chrome tape** (or chrome striping tape), available from an auto parts store

To assemble your kaleidoscope, cover the three pieces of cardboard with the chrome tape and trim them back to the 4 × 1½ size. Then, put them together into a triangle so that their longer sides connect and with the chrome on the inside, and tape them together. Insert the triangle into the center of the toilet paper roll; when you look through the roll, you should see the shiny sides.

Now, take your two bead containers and remove their lids. Place a few beads in one, then screw its lid back on. On top of this container, screw the bottom of the second container. You won't need the other lid. Instead, insert the toilet paper roll into the second container until it hits the bottom. Now you can look through your kaleidoscope while turning it and get a bug's eye view of your world. If you want some variety to your kaleidoscope, try changing your beads or experimenting with other items like paper clips.

WORDS to KNOW

compound eye: Many insects and some crustaceans have compound eyes. Regular eyes receive one big image; compound eyes receive many little images and then put them together into one complete picture. Although an insect's eye may not focus well from a great distance, its vision is excellent up close.

What does a bee say when he comes back to the hive?

Hi, Honey, I'm home!

Hiding in a Honeycomb

There are six bugs hiding in this honeycomb. Can you find them? Start at any letter and move one space at a time in any direction. Once you've found all the bugs, see what other words you can make.

How do fire flies start a race?
"Ready, set, GLOW!"

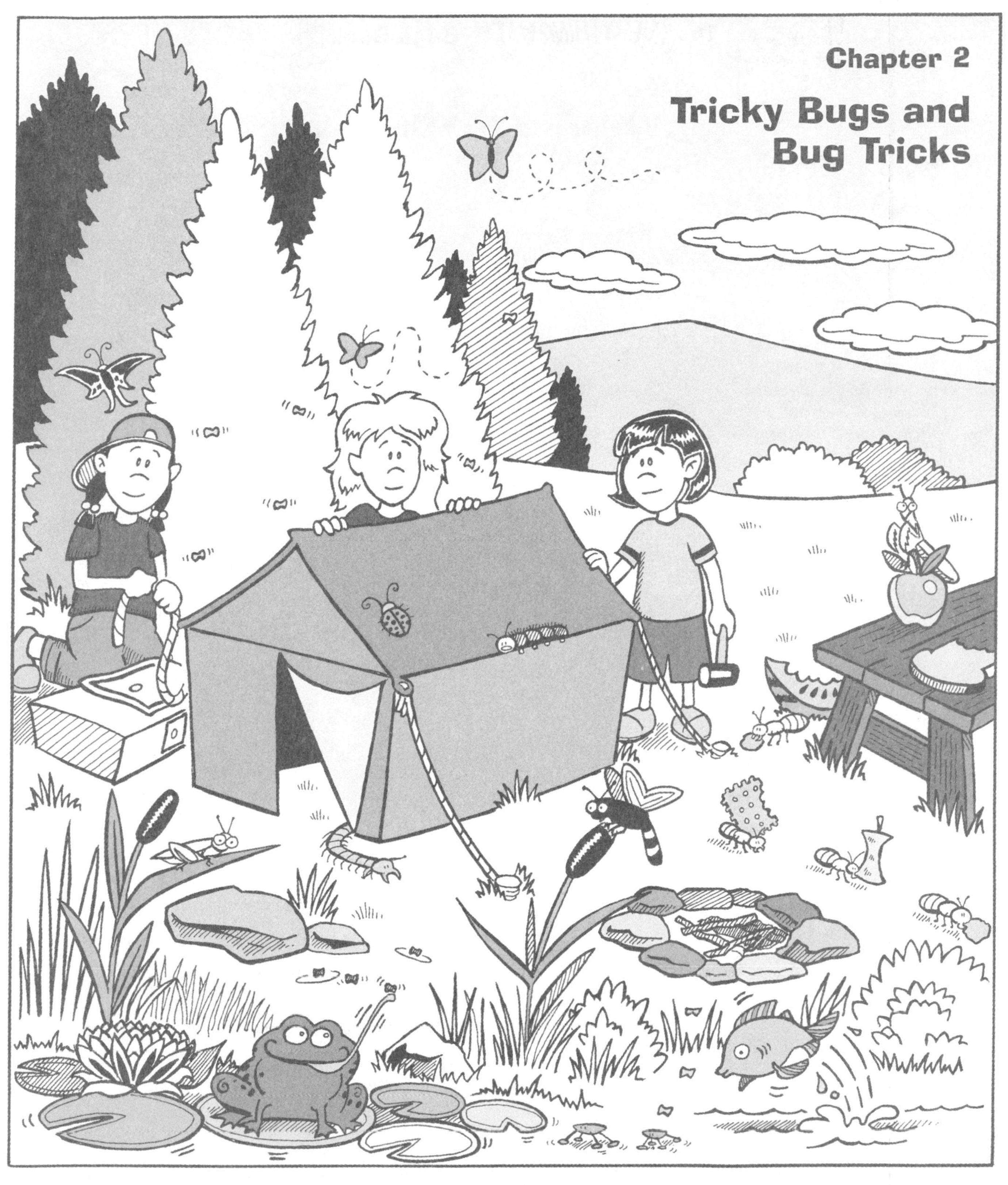
Chapter 2
Tricky Bugs and Bug Tricks

Welcome to the Miniature Circus!

Ladies and gentlemen, boys and girls, children of all ages! Welcome to the Greatest Bug Show on Earth. A show where you can fascinate your family and friends with the amazing tricks that your trained insects can do. Well, okay, maybe they're not *really* trained. As a matter of fact, they're not actually trained at all!

To hold your own circus, all you need to do is get yourself a few newly caught black beetles, ladybugs, and caterpillars. Your animal acts will need only a few props, like a Ping-Pong ball with a small amount of honey or something sticky on it (for the beetles to walk on), a rope (for the ladybugs to climb), and a balance beam (for the caterpillars to cross).

FUN FACT

A Jumpin' Act

Fleas have been entertaining audiences for the last 200 years in Europe and North America. These wingless creatures are so little, they could fit on the head of a pin, and yet, they are able to jump as high as 13 inches and move objects weighing 400 times their own size.

It's a Flea Circus

What if you're not into making ladybugs or caterpillars perform? Well, there are always fleas! Finding fleas is easy; all you need is a dog or a cat. If your family doesn't have a pet, see if your neighbors do—but don't make this into a case of dognapping or catnapping—ask the animal's owner first.

Once you find a fully consenting pet that is willing to let you get up close (good luck!), search through its fur, looking for a flea. When you find one, you need to move quickly—pinch it between your finger and thumb. Don't be afraid of squishing it. A flea's exoskeleton (a shell, the insect version of a skeleton that is *outside* of its body) is so hard, it can actually survive

▶ Try This
A Construction Project

If you really want to go all out, you can construct an entire amusement park of rides with one box of toothpicks and a bag of miniature marshmallows. This is where your imagination comes in. Simple props such as a balance beam or dumbbells can be made from a single toothpick with a marshmallow on each end. But, for those of you who like a challenge, you can attempt more difficult acts with your bugs, by making seesaws, ladders for the high dive, or even a Ferris wheel.

being stepped on. Now, all you need is a small leash, about the size of a piece of your hair, to tie on the flea.

A well-trained flea will stick around without a leash and only requires one thing—food. Unfortunately, fleas only eat one thing—blood. That's why they make their homes in the fur of animals, so that they have a steady supply of food any time they like.

Forget about getting those kinds of treats for your fleas. After the circus is over, you can release them in the wild and they'll find food for themselves. But how about preparing some circus treats for your audience? You may want to provide the usual: peanuts, popcorn, cotton candy, or snow cones. Or maybe you'll decide to serve something unusual, like "Edible Bugs on a Ball."

And of course a circus cannot be complete without the animals, so don't forget the circus train. You'll be the talk of the town when everyone sees your boxed train carrying zebra swallowtails, stilt bugs, gypsy moths, snakeflies, elephant beetles, or any other bugs with a circus name.

Who Am I?

I could be very useful to a circus. But most of the time I'm up in a tree. My babies like to spin silk to make their home. Our houses are usually found in the fork of a fruit tree. Look for me in a tree that is missing its leaves—you'll probably find my family there, finishing our lunch! **Who am I?**

(A tent caterpillar)

Warning!

You can set up the greatest show on earth, but you can't do it alone! You will need some help from adults to organize the event and supervise the games. Just think—they can help you set up the booths, buy supplies and prizes, and then award trophies and gifts at the end of the fair.

The Big Show

If the circus comes only but once a year (or so the saying goes), why not go all out and prepare a large circus event or even a fair in your neighborhood? Invite your friends to help you host it. Perhaps you can pick an occasion to celebrate—the beginning of summer, Halloween, or maybe even your birthday.

No one can resist throwing darts at the Darting Bugs booth or mixing his or her own flavors at the Snow Cone booth. Or how about trying to put out the Fire Ant at the squirt-gun firing range. Maybe your favorite one will be the Bug Tattoo booth or the Bug Face Painting tent. Or perhaps you'll look forward to playing at the Fly Swatting booth. If you're really brave, you can have a Fly-in-the-Pie "pie in the face" booth or contest. And for the younger visitors to your circus or fair, you can provide floating Bug Eggs with prizes inside.

Sounds too difficult? Don't get discouraged! All you need is your imagination, an adult to supervise you, and the following materials.

Darting Bugs

This game requires a couple of darts, a large appliance box (to tape the bug-decorated balloons into), and an adult to act

What kind of bees are always fighting?

Rumble bees!

▶ Try This

Edible Bugs on a Ball

To make Edible Bugs on a Ball treats, you take a large marshmallow, roll it in peanut butter, and then sprinkle it in your choice of "bugs"—chocolate chips, raisins, jimmies, or other candies.

as a judge. Then, contestants take turns throwing darts at the bug balloons. The winner is the contestant who nails down more bugs!

Snow Cones

Get some crushed ice (ask an adult to crush it in a blender), paper cups, spoons, and several flavors of juice or flavored drinks in squirt bottles or cups. Then, all you need is some ice in a cup to decorate with flavored juice!

Fire Ant

What you need for this booth is a candle decorated with the picture of an ant, one stand to place it on, and two or more squirt guns filled with water to try to squirt the flame out. Then, draw a line where the contestants need to stand, and find an adult to act as a judge. The object of the game is to be the one to extinguish the candle's flame.

ringmaster: A person who introduces and is in charge of the acts in the rings of a circus. This person usually wears a top hat and a tuxedo with tails. At almost every single circus performance, the ringmaster will begin with a dramatic welcome: "Ladieeeessss and Gentlemen . . . Welcome to the greatest (or smallest) show on earth!"

What's the Difference?

To solve this puzzle, figure out where to put the scrambled letters. They all fit in spaces under their own column. When you have correctly filled in the grid, you will have the answer to the riddle.

HINT: The letters only form words horizontally. Use each letter only once.

What's the difference between a coyote and a flea?

~~O~~	T	E		~~R~~		~~W~~		Y								
T	N	E		R	A	P	R	~~O~~		~~O~~			O	~~H~~		
O	R	~~A~~	I	H	I	E	R	A	W	O	S		T	E		
P	H	H	E	H	O	~~I~~	L	S	N	L	N	T	H	N	E	
O			■			W			■			■		H		■
		A					■			D	■				■	■
				R	■			O				■			■	■
			■			I			■	■	■	■	■	■	■	■

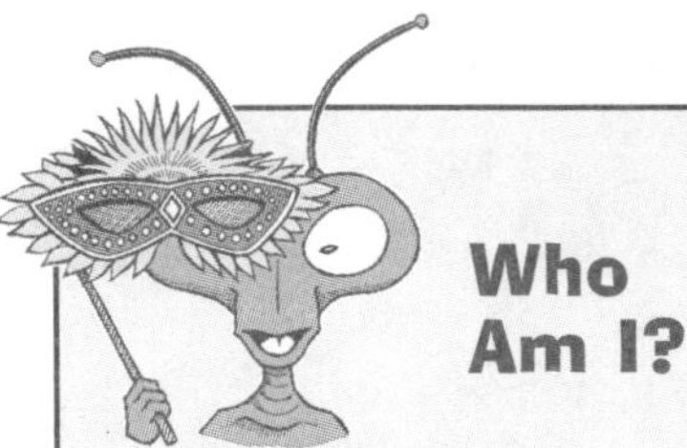

Who Am I?

I am one of the many kinds of flies that live in the water. My legs are shaped like a scoop, so I could be very handy at a construction site—I could lift things up and move them around . . . or so you would think if you knew my name. **Who am I?**

(A crane fly)

Bug Tattoo

Here's how you can make bug tattoos. Get small squares of white paper and draw bugs on them with water-based "washable" markers. Then, use a damp washcloth to moisten your skin and hold the picture of the bug against your skin until someone counts to fifteen—and you've got your very own homemade bug tattoo!

Bug Face Painting

This one is even easier. All you need is an artist, a few paint brushes, watercolor paints that are washable, a cup of water to rinse the brushes, a couple of paper towels, and a few bug pictures that you can use as samples. Visitors to the Bug Face Painting booth can pick from one of the samples (or give an idea of their own) and the artist will paint the picture on their faces.

Fly Swatting

The object of this game is to swat (hit) the "fly" (a sock filled with rice that you can hang on a string from a tree limb or a clothesline) with a fly swatter. To make the game more difficult, try to hang it up so that kids would have to jump to hit the fly. Or, you can blindfold them or spin them around before they take their turn. Those who manage to swat the fly may be rewarded with party favors or little goodie bags filled with candy.

Fly in the Pie

You will need a box or two of the wafer cookies, a can of spray whipping cream, and several "hungry" volunteers. Prepare your fly pies by spraying several cookies with whipping cream and setting them on plates. Then, the volunteers must eat their pie without using their hands. If you choose to have this game, make sure you are prepared for the mess—a water hose to clean up the mess is essential. It's also a good idea to have your contestants wear "uniforms" made out of garbage bags!

Bug Eggs

Purchase some plastic eggs and take some time to fill them with small prizes that are safe for even the youngest kids. Then, set the eggs afloat in a small tub or pool, and find an adult to supervise the little kids who will go egg hunting in your Bug Eggs booth.

Bug Races

If you like being fast and enjoy racing, this is the game for you. To start your bug races, you'll need to collect the following supplies:

- **Several different bugs** (you can race two of the same kind of insects or two completely different types); try to find the fastest bug to race against your friends' bugs.
- **Masking tape** (to mark your lanes and finish lines)
- A smooth surface, like a **table**, to be used for racing
- **Ribbons and prizes** (for the winners)
- **Trays of mud** (for tough-terrain competitions)
- **Two pieces of string** (to be held at an uphill angle by four people, one on each end for the bugs to climb)
- **A stopwatch** (if you want to see how fast your bug is or if you want to take turns racing your bugs and want to know which one is faster)

What legendary insect is covered with fur, has big teeth, and lives high in the mountains?

Bug Foot!

FUN FACT

The Bug Olympics

Did you know people have been racing bugs for some time now? That's how they know which insects hold the current record for being the fastest, slowest, highest-flying, and so on. The fastest insect to date is the dragonfly. It can reach flight speeds of 60 miles per hour—that's fast enough to get you a speeding ticket!

Why are mosquitoes most annoying at night?

They like to grab a bite before they go to sleep!

Set your multilegged contestants at the START line, and with a wave of your green flag, they're off! If you keep score, you can hold whole tournaments where the winners race each other until you find your racing champion. What do you think would be a good bug-racing prize to award the winner?

Muddy Dauber Relays

If you're looking for a game where you can compete against your friends, try organizing a mud relay race where you relay a muddy dauber down a line of people. A real mud dauber is a kind of wasp. In your game, however, a muddy dauber is a long water-filled balloon.

Here is how the relay will work. Divide all contestants into two teams and line them up in two lines. The object of the relay is to be the first team to pass the muddy dauber from one end of the line to the other. To make the game more interesting, each contestant should dip his or her hands in "mud"—chocolate pudding! After the relay is over, have a sprinkler party to wash off all the "mud."

The Grasshopper Egg Relay

Here is another idea for a fun relay game. Ask your parents to prepare some hard-boiled eggs. (If you have the time, it's fun to color them or decorate them with pictures or stickers of grasshoppers.) Then, divide all the contestants into pairs. Each pair receives one egg. When the relay begins, each pair tosses the egg back and forth. Each time an egg is cracked or broken, the pair who broke it is eliminated from the game, so that eventually all you have left are two contestants. The last person to not break an egg wins!

Smart Bugs Code

These bugs are trying to tell you something! Use the decoder to figure out the answer to the riddle.

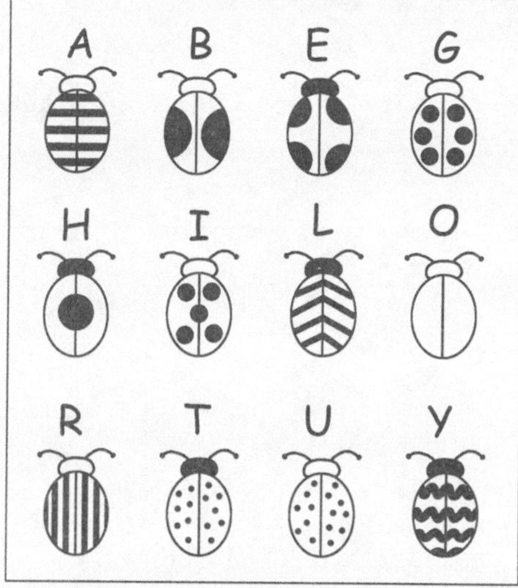

What do you say to a firefly when he gets 100% on his math test?

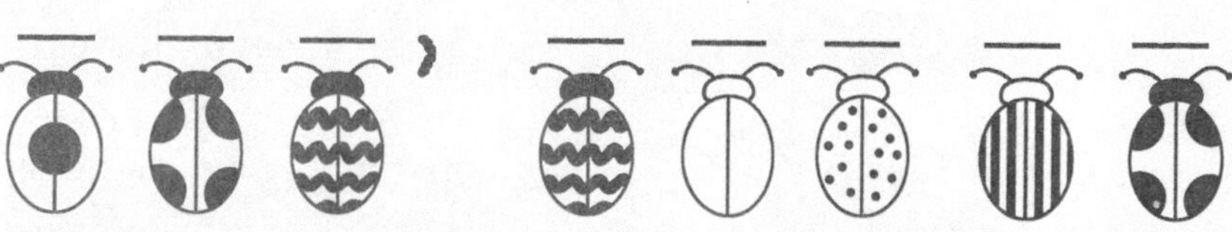

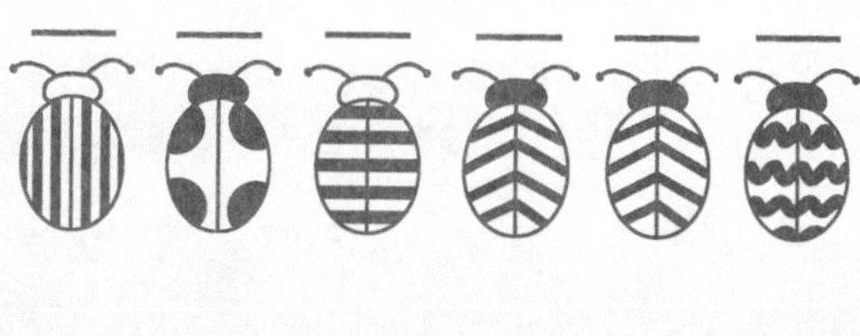

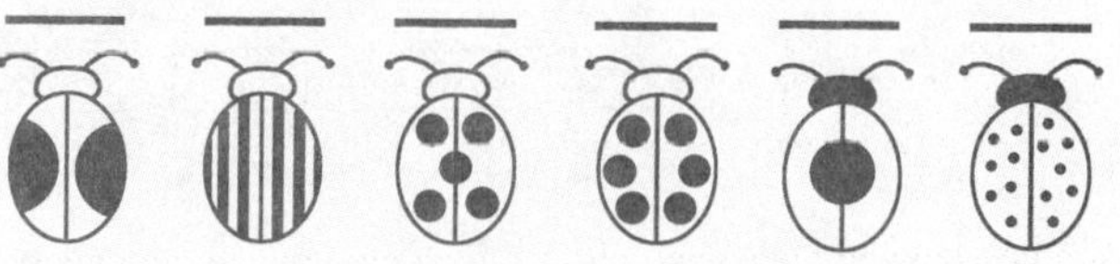

Who Am I?

I live along the shores of streams and ponds. If you watch closely, you may see me hopping from place to place. My big bulgy eyes and the bumps all over me might look sort of familiar to you. If so, be careful not to touch me, if you believe in that whole "wart" thing. **Who am I?**

(A toad bug)

Water Bug Toss

Use a marker to decorate several water balloons to look like bugs. Then, find a couple of big old towels that no one would mind you use. If there are only two of you playing, each person holds on to one end of the towel by the corners. Then, one person tosses one of the water-bug balloons high up into the air and the two of you try to catch it with the towel. If you have four or more players, two of you can try to toss the water bugs over to the other team with the towel to see if they can catch it.

Train for the Marathon

Okay, so maybe you can't complete the entire marathon—not yet, anyway, but how about a running race? Host your marathon in a park or a schoolyard, and invite other kids from the neighborhood to participate. You can make running numbers for each runner and provide water and energy drinks for them. And of course, don't forget to set up the start and the finish lines. Once everything is ready, the runners can line up at the start line; once you blow the whistle, they are off and racing!

Bubble-Blowing Beetles

Now, here's a trick for you. Did you know that some bugs can blow bubbles? Diving beetles, which live underwater, breathe out the air they extract from the water with their gills by blowing bubbles. And spittle bugs blow so many bubbles around themselves you may not even know they are there.

These bugs are hard to catch, especially if you don't live anywhere near a pond, but you can make your own spittle bugs—it's easy. First, you place a straw halfway inside of a balloon. Then, tape the end of the balloon to the straw. To make the spittle mixture, combine 1 tablespoon of dish soap to 1 cup of water. When you are ready, blow the balloon up by blowing through the straw. Pinch the end of the straw closed until you are ready to place the end of the straw into the "spittle mixture." Then, let the straw open and watch what happens.

WORDS to KNOW

marathon: A long-distance race that requires runners to complete 26.2 miles. Although some runners run for speed, for many others the real challenge is in finishing the race. Marathons date all the way back to Ancient Greece, when a messenger from the town of Marathon had to run for 26.2 miles in order to carry news of a military victory to Athens.

Vacuum Bubbles

We wonder who made the amazing discovery that you can suspend a ball in the air by placing it above the tube of a canister vacuum (a small vacuum with two openings—one that blows air out of its hose and another that takes it in). And guess what—you can recreate this amazing magic act of levitation (which means to cause an object to float in the air) at home, especially if you've got younger siblings or cousins to entertain.

What is a bug's favorite sport?
Mothball!

▸ Try This
Bubblegum-Blowing Contest

When's the last time you held a Bubblegum-Blowing Contest? Whether you challenge your brothers or sisters, or your mom or dad, you may be surprised at who can blow the biggest bubble. All you need in order to hold the contest are four things: gum, a ruler, peanut butter (to remove any stray gum), and—of course—the contestants. Now, start blowing!

The first thing you need to do is find an adult who can help you get the vacuum and make sure that the vacuum and the vacuum hose are clean (the vacuum bag should be removed). Then, ask the adult to make sure that the vacuum hose is hooked to the "out" vent. Once everything is ready, turn the vacuum on to be sure the air is coming out of the tube. Then, try placing several different balls in the air's path above the hose. You can experiment with Ping-Pong balls, beach balls, pom-pom balls, or any other balls you might have lying around the house.

You can also use the vacuum for bubble play, by letting the hose blow air through a strainer, a funnel, a bath scrubby, and other items from around your house that are dipped in a bubble solution (1 tablespoons of dish soap for every 1 cup of water). Again, don't play with the vacuum on your own—wait until one of your parents or another adult gets home and helps you out.

What has four wheels and flies?

A garbage truck!

▶ Try This

Make a Spittle Sundae Surprise

No, don't spit on your friends' sundaes! You can make bug spittle by mixing sherbet or ice cream with lemon/lime soda (soft drink) and adding a few bugs (jellybeans or bubblegum balls work nicely for this) into the mix.

Chapter 3

Under Construction: Bug Builders

Busy as a Bee

Help this busy bee to collect nectar from all the white flowers. He must go from START to END and visit each white flower only once. He can fly up, down, left, and right, but not diagonally. The bee cannot fly over or land on any dark flowers.

HINT: Try making practice paths on a thin piece of tracing paper placed over the puzzle.

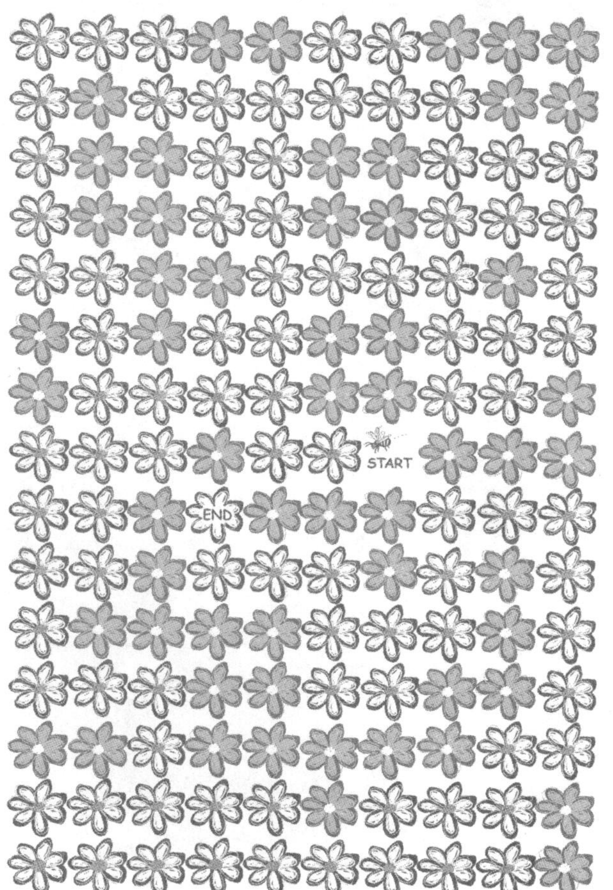

Wasps and Spitballs

What do wasps have to do with spitballs? Well, if you've ever made a spitball, you know that by chewing up a piece of paper you change it into a whole new object. Of course, the only reason kids make spitballs is to spit them at someone or something, which usually gets them in trouble. Well, wasps make spitballs too, but they have a much better reason for doing that. They actually use their spitballs to make wasp nests.

A wasp's paper nest is actually made out of small bits of chewed-up wood and saliva. Other wasps prefer to build their homes out of mud or in the ground. No matter where you find them, wasps will protect their homes, and the way they defend them is by stinging, so don't get too close!

Wasps and bees may have been the first inventors of fans and air conditioning. As temperatures soar outside, you will find the bees and wasps fanning their homes with their wings. The fast movement of their wings cools the nest, making it more comfortable for the queen and the eggs that have not hatched yet.

Dissecting a Honeycomb

Aren't you curious to see what a honeycomb really looks like and what's on the inside? There is a way to find out!

The best thing to do is to buy a honeycomb at the grocery store. Then take the honeycomb and place it on a plate or cookie sheet. Look at it closely. Once you've examined the comb, here comes the sticky part—cutting into it. The honeycomb's cells are made of wax, each one filled with honey. Each cell in the comb has six sides to it. These six-sided cells are known as *hexagons*.

FUN FACT

Food for Thought

Bees collect nectar from flowers. As they fly from one flower to the other, they spread the flowers' pollen, which allows them to germinate into the fruits and vegetables we eat each day.

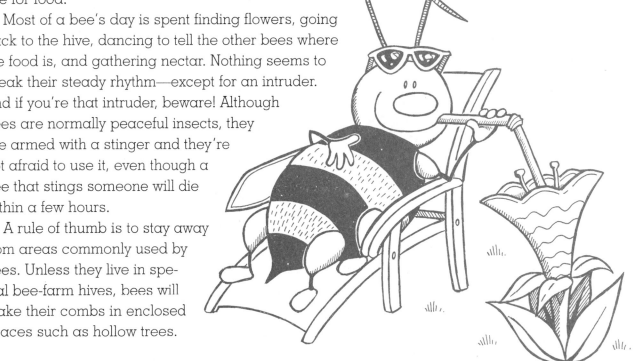

A Honey of a Builder

Bees! They're everywhere you go, unless of course you're at the North or South Pole. Bees aren't very fond of the cold. They need the warm sun to survive.

Another thing that bees need is nectar, which they use for food.

Most of a bee's day is spent finding flowers, going back to the hive, dancing to tell the other bees where the food is, and gathering nectar. Nothing seems to break their steady rhythm—except for an intruder. And if you're that intruder, beware! Although bees are normally peaceful insects, they are armed with a stinger and they're not afraid to use it, even though a bee that stings someone will die within a few hours.

A rule of thumb is to stay away from areas commonly used by bees. Unless they live in special bee-farm hives, bees will make their combs in enclosed spaces such as hollow trees.

The Bee's Best Weapon

The bee normally keeps its stinger inside of its body, but takes it out if it is frightened or feels it must defend its home. The stinger, which has barbs on it, hooks into the flesh of the intruder and releases a poison into the wound. Scraping the stinger off quickly will stop the flow of poison.

Making Paper-Nest Paper

Making paper similar to the type that wasps use for their nests is fairly easy to do. First, you will want to locate some old paper (brightly colored, non-shiny paper works best). Tear the paper into 1-inch squares and let them soak for a few hours in a bowl filled with enough water to cover them. Then, find an old blender to blend the paper mixture until it forms a paste.

If your paper paste seems too dry, you can add a little more water. If it seems too soupy, add a few more paper squares. Now you can also add decorations, such as flowers, threads or confetti.

Pour out your "new" paper onto a glass plate or tray, squishing it flat or mounding it like a nest. Professional paper makers use square frames with screens attached to them to squeeze out all of the extra water and flatten the pulp into a sheet. You can also use this paper paste for sculpting piñatas, puppet heads, statues, and lots of other fun things.

Mind Your own Beeswax

Wax is very important to bees—it's great for building places to store honey! But people have a lot of uses for beeswax, too. Use the following word equations to sound out the name of three popular products that contain beeswax.

▶ Try This

Make a Bug Piñata

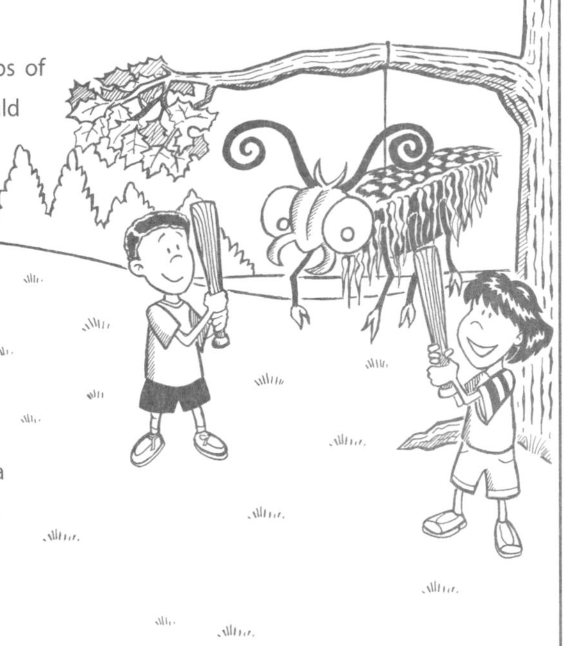

Take a balloon, blow it up, and cover it with strips of paper dipped in plain white glue. A few layers should be good enough. Place the covered balloon on a cookie sheet lined with wax paper to dry. If the balloon hasn't popped already by the time the piñata is dry, pop it!

Now it's time to turn your balloon into a bug. You can add crêpe paper streamers for the legs and cut paper decorations for the eyes. When it is time for the party, ask one of your parents or another adult to cut a whole at the top of the piñata so that you can fill it with your favorite candy. Then, you can hang it from a beam or a tree limb with a piece of string. Using a plastic bat, the blindfolded partygoers take turns trying to break it open.

The Walking Stick

No, a walking stick really isn't a stick that can walk. And it's not a cane to help you walk, either. It's a bug! Walking sticks do look like sticks, and for a very good reason—that's how they hide. In fact, their disguise works so well, these creatures have been around for more than 4 million years.

Not all bugs have remained the same for so long. As time passes, many bugs have mutated in order to adapt to their new surroundings. People adapt over time too! Take your messy room for example. You have probably adapted to it. (Your parents, on the other hand, probably never will.)

mutate: To change form. Over time, many insect species have mutated into new kinds of bugs. To adapt to an ever-changing planet, certain bugs have learned to eat everything from fabrics to pepper. Many have slowly adapted to temperatures ranging from freezing to burning hot—120 degrees Fahrenheit, to be exact.

Living Life on the Edge

A walking stick spends most of its day in a balancing act of survival. Imagine avoiding hungry birds, pretending you're a stick anytime someone comes around, and hanging on for dear life when a storm comes. It sort of makes you appreciate how much easier it is to be a person.

If you're still curious what it feels like to be a walking stick, try walking a balance beam. For beginners, the best beam is a regular 2 × 4 board. Lay the board flat on its 4-inch side (for those of you who are carpenters, it's actually only 3½ inches long). With some practice you should be able to advance to the 2-inch side (which is really only 1½ inches). This requires bracing the beam with 8-inch pieces of board screwed on to each end to keep the beam from tipping over (ask your parents to help you out with this).

Once you've mastered the balance beam, it's time to add a few more things, creating an obstacle course. If you are inside, you can use items like pillows, cushions, tables, footstools, blankets, or anything else you want to crawl through, in, on, or over. Moving outdoors allows for small slides, big boxes, planks, tires, and more. There's no limit to the obstacles you can add, so be creative, but keep everyone's safety in mind!

What kind of bug can fly without wings?
A fris-bee!

FUN FACT

What's in a Name?

Almost all insects have two names. One is its scientific name, which is made up of two words that are usually very long and hard to pronounce. The other is the common name or nickname. For example, a common honey-bee's scientific name is *Apis mellifera.* An insect's name can tell you a lot about it. For example, an inchworm will inch its way across a leaf and the click beetle really does make a clicking sound.

Stilt Bugs

Tired of seeing the world from just your point of view? Try seeing it from about 2 feet higher. By making a pair a stilts you can turn yourself into a stilt bug. There are actually two kinds of stilt bugs—the "regular" stilt bugs and the stilt-legged flies. Both insects tend to walk over other bugs, which could be especially bad if you are a squash bug!

Metamorphosis

Sometimes a bug starts out looking one way (a creepy green caterpillar) and ends up looking completely different (a brown and white moth). Words can do that, too!

Start at the first word and find a path through the grid by combining two words that go together to make a new word or phrase. You can travel up and down, or side to side, but not diagonally. Use the end of one word or phrase as the beginning of the next. Be careful—some paths will lead you nowhere!

I used to be one of YOU!
What are you?

START

butter	dish	towel	bar	bell
fly	wheel	chair	man	hole
paper	clip	bottom	less	on
back	door	bell	knob	top
fire	fly	trap	door	secret

END

Stilts come in all shapes and sizes. Clowns and dancers have used them for years. You can start low, and then work your way up to higher and fancier stilt stunts. Try practicing walking around above the ground with stilts made of shoeboxes filled with smaller firm boxes.

Shoebox Stilts

To make the shoebox stilts, you will need two shoeboxes, two cords, and material for filling the shoeboxes. First, take one shoebox and cut two holes on the bottom, so that if you were to step into the box, one hole would be to the right of your foot and the other to the left. Insert the cord into one hole and through the other, so that you can pick up the shoebox by pulling at the two ends of the cord. Then, fill the shoebox with hard material, such as other boxes, lots of newspaper, or pieces of wood. Make two holes in the top of the shoebox so that you can pull the ends of the cord out once you close the shoebox, and then tape the top of the shoebox shut. Tie the two ends of the cord together. Do the same with the other shoebox. Now you can step on top of your shoebox stilts and use the two cord circles to keep them under your feet as you walk.

After you have mastered the shoeboxes, you can move on to coffee cans or taller boxes. To advance even further, you can consult the Web for how to make even higher stilts. Just type the words "making stilts" into the search box and see where the search engine will take you. There are several stilt-making sites to choose from.

Watch Out!

The best place to walk on shoebox stilts is a grassy area—the softer the ground, the better. Walking on stilts is not as easy as it looks! Even the best stilt walker will tell you to prepare for falling off.

▶ Try This

A-maze-ing!

Mole crickets dig tunnels that are a lot like mazes, only underground. Maybe you would like to test the maze skills of a real bug? You can make your own maze out of heavy cardboard and glue. The base of the maze can be any size you like. The sides of the maze are made from strips of cardboard or pieces of wood, glued to the base in a maze pattern. Remember, the maze should have an entrance and an exit, plus a few dead ends. Once you've constructed your maze and it's dry, test it out with a few black beetles or any insect of your choice.

Who Am I?

You may have seen my shield-shaped body before. Some members of my family are dull-colored bugs and others are very bright. Most of us like to eat plants. But a few of us like to eat other animals. For dessert, we like fruit. Most people don't like us—they think we . . . smell! **Who am I?**

(A stink bug)

Mole Crickets and Cave Mazes

Are you afraid of the dark? Most people are, even if they won't admit it. Imagine if you loved the dark. Some insects do, and a mole cricket is one of them. Because they like the dark, mole crickets are seldom seen, unless you happen to be digging in the ground where they live.

Mole crickets use their shovel-like legs to dig their nests and to find buried food.

FUN FACT

From Egg to Bug

Once an insect lays an egg, one of three things will happen to it, depending on what bug it belongs to. The egg may hatch into a miniature adult, molting and growing until it reaches its full size (that's called "simple growth"). It may hatch into a wingless nymph that changes into a winged adult with its last molting (that's called "incomplete metamorphosis"). Or, the egg changes into a larva, then into a pupa, and then—finally—a fully-grown adult emerges. This is called "complete metamorphosis."

Tongue Twister

Try saying this three times fast!
Big black bug's blood

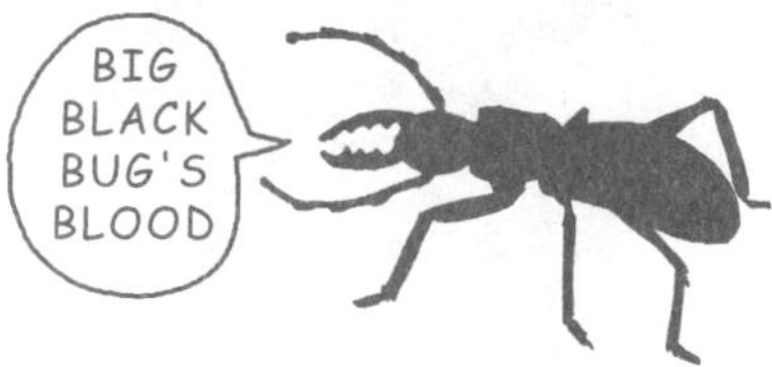

They eat earthworms and other insects found underground. A mother mole cricket is very protective of her young. Once her eggs are laid she stays with them until they hatch.

If you are looking for a game that can test your friends' skills, try a magnetic maze. Find a smooth paper plate and draw your maze on top (a permanent marker will work best). Then, follow the marker lines this time with a bead of white glue. For heavy lines you may want to apply several coats of glue, one at a time as they dry. The bug you race can be made from a metal washer—decorate it with a bug sticker or a cutout. Using a fairly strong magnet on the underside of the plate, you can "race" the bug through the maze, to see who can get to the end fastest.

Labyrinth Fun

A labyrinth is pretty much the same thing as a maze, but for people. In the days of knights and castles, labyrinths were used to keep out intruders. Strangers or invaders would soon lose their way through the labyrinth's winding paths, never to reach the castle. Smaller versions of these mazes can still be found in some castle gardens.

For fun, you can create you own labyrinth using clotheslines and sheets. Hang the sheets along the line to go one direction, then across to the other line to change the path. Mazes for children can also be made in cornfields and out of hay bales stacked to form the walls. One way to make your own maze is to use large boxes. By removing one or two sides and putting the different sections together, back to side and so on, you can make openings or dead ends. Scary labyrinths work well for fall parties or overnighters. If you can use your basement or yard, put your maze together by day, then have your friends try to go through it by night, using flashlights.

A Miner Maze

Another type of maze is a mine. Miners exist both in the insect world and in ours. Human miners go underground to search for precious metals and other substances that don't exist on the earth's surface. Insects known as leaf miners burrow inside leafs to look for things they need. These microscopic creatures are actually young moths and flies that hatch out of eggs laid by their parents on leaves.

The next time you look closely at a leaf, if you see a snake-like pattern on it, those are the tunnels made by the leaf miners. When you go for a walk sometime, try stopping to look at the leaves. All kinds of insects lay their eggs on the leaves of plants and trees.

Who Am I?

I am a worm that turns into a moth. When I am full-grown, I have a thick body with spotted wings that span about 2 inches. My family name is *Cossidae*. I am from the *Lepidoptera* order of insects. You might expect to see me carrying a toolbox. **Who am I?**

(A carpenter moth/worm)

Hidden Beauty

METAMORPHOSIS

Can you believe that a delicate butterfly might have started its life as a big, fat caterpillar? That's what metamorphosis is all about! How many little words can you find hiding inside the big word metamorphosis? Bet you can find more than fifty!

DIRECTIONS: Each letter can only be used as many times as it appears in the big word. For example, you can spell a word like ROOT, because there are two Os in METAMORPHOSIS. You can't spell TOOT, because there is only one T.

Tunneling with Mole Crickets

Some insects like the dark, and a mole cricket is one of them. Because of this, mole crickets are seldom seen, unless you happen to be digging in the ground where they live. These "mole" imposters use their shovel-like legs to dig their nests and to find buried food. They eat earthworms and other insects found underground. A mother mole cricket is very protective of her young. Once her eggs are laid, she stays with them the entire time, not leaving them until they hatch.

Can you help this mama mole cricket get to her eggs?

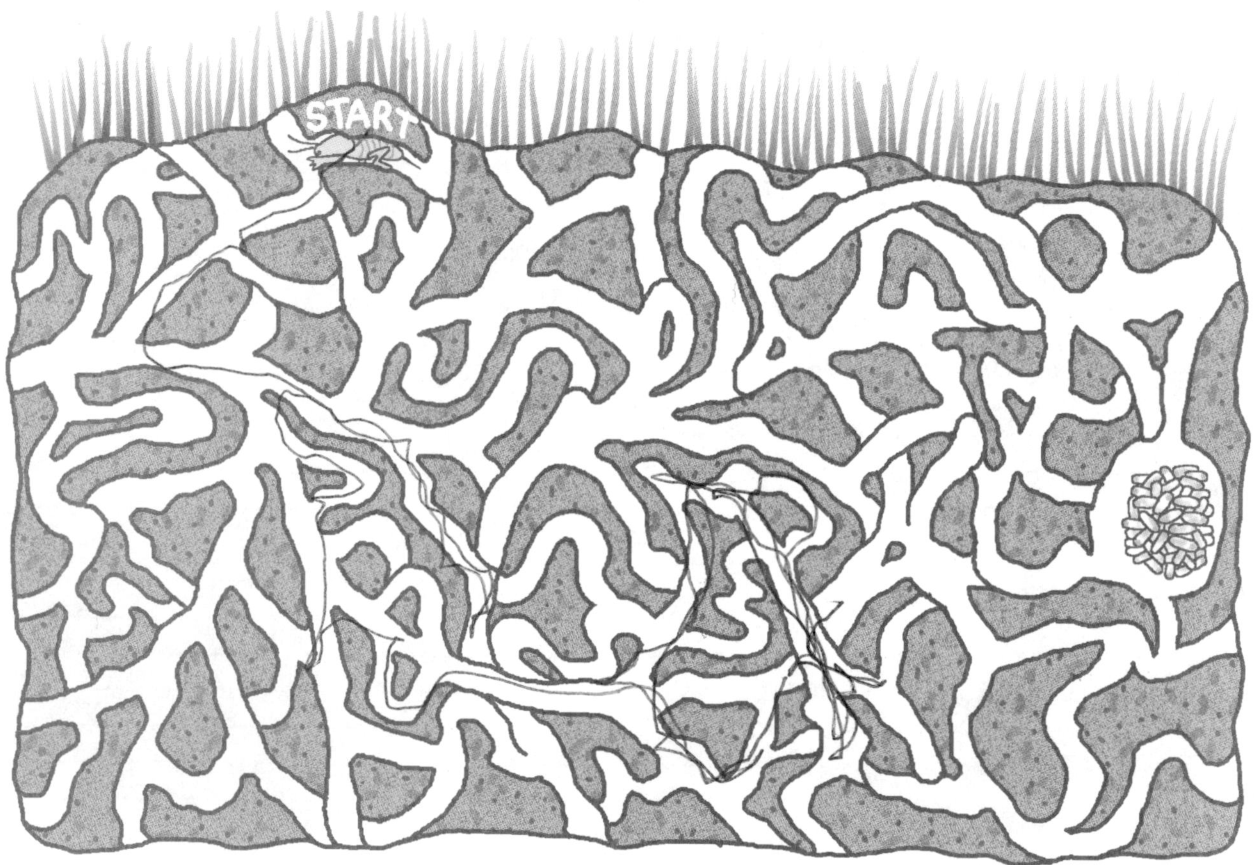

Chapter 4

Demolition Bugs

Termites and Destruction

FUN FACT

Long Live the Queen!

A queen termite is much bigger than the rest of the termites and can grow to be as large as 3 inches long, which is several times larger than the king termite. She can also live for a long time—up to fifty years. During that time, she is only responsible for one thing: laying eggs, millions of them.

You're walking across a floor that you've walked across hundreds of times before, when suddenly a board falls in and you discover you have termites. These demolition experts prey on unsuspecting homeowners who seldom ever see them until it's too late. So, why do they want to eat you out of your home? It's simple, really—they're hungry.

Picture yourself as a termite. It's after school, you're starving, and you see a piping hot chocolate chip cookie just lying there. What would you do? Termites eat wood and make tunnels within wooden boards to build their homes. Because they spend much of their time underground, most termites are light in color and have no wings. Termites are actually quite small, about the size of a grain of rice. Soldier termites protect the nest by shooting a nasty fluid out of their snout at anyone who tries to enter it. And worker termites care for the needs of the queen, the king, and the baby termites.

We can learn a lot about construction and destruction from a termite. Through our relationship with termites, we have learned what makes a structure weak and what makes it strong. To test this knowledge firsthand, you will need two large blocks of Styrofoam. Try standing on one. If it's big enough, it should be able to support you. Now take the other block and with the help of a parent, poke several holes all over it with a long nail or a drill (this will make a mess, so taking your experiment outside is a very good idea).

▶ Try This
Sun Time

Did you know you can use shadows to tell time? Take a paper plate and place it face down on your lawn. Poke a plastic knife through the center into the ground. Every hour, mark your plate sundial clock with a number for the time where the shadow falls. The next day, you will be able to tell what time it is by the location of the shadow—unless of course it's cloudy that day.

What do you get when you cross an insect with a computer?

Bug bytes!

Now try to stand on this block again. What happens? The block crumbles under pressure. And that's what happens when termites tunnel back and forth through the wood. If they are not stopped, they'll eat it all up, leaving nothing but a pile of wood dust.

In sandy places, termites are forced to build their homes out of dirt and sand. Some of these homes reach as high as 30 feet. These termite towers throw large shadows that could be used as sundials. Termites will also tunnel great distances underground to find wood. If a termite sees sunlight, it will die within a few hours. Termites require moisture and darkness in order to survive.

At the Construction Site

You can also test your construction skills by using boxes or blocks of wood. First, try building a solid wall or tower. Then, set something on top to see if the wall can support it. Next, build a wall or tower with a few spaces in between your blocks. Will it still support the same object this time?

FUN FACT

Architectural Design

Architects make small models of buildings before the construction workers actually begin working on the real thing, to see if the design will work. You can do so too by building small buildings out of graham crackers and frosting. The best part of this construction project is that you can eat it when you're through!

Who Am I?

I love to eat clothes. You can usually find me in your closet, where I hide on your sweater by disguising myself with little pieces of wool all over my body. Although I don't use one, my name has part of the word "suitcase" in it. **Who am I?**

(A case-bearing clothes moth)

Try building a pyramid tower out of paper cups. Place the cups on their rims to make the first row. Stack the second row by placing each cup half way over the bottom two, the same way as bricks are laid. Can you remove a cup from the center and have the pyramid remain standing? How about building a pyramid of people? What happens if someone leaves or weakens the lower levels of the structure?

What else do you think you can construct? With your parent's help, think of something you would like to build and then try it. Who knows, you might invent something that will improve the lives of millions of people!

At the Demolition Site

If you want to destroy something, you probably have to build it first. Then, you have to consider your demolition strategy. It's not as random as you might think. Demolition experts will tell you, it's very important to know where to weaken a structure, so it will fall in the right direction. That's how they can blow up a building, without harming the building standing next to it. One food you can construct and then demolish with a few of your friends is the Termite Surprise. Here's what you'll need to make it:

- 3 packages of **graham crackers**
- 1 bowl of **tapioca pudding**
- 1 tub of **whipped cream**

Line a cake pan with one package of the graham crackers, laying them out side by side like boards. Cover this layer with the tapioca pudding. Take the second package of graham crackers and crush them into what looks like sawdust. Sprinkle the crumbs on the pudding and then cover this with a layer of

Where do they send a sick insect?

To the wasp-ital!

whipped cream. Lay the last package of crackers over the top. Refrigerate your creation for a few hours and then serve—and let the demolition begin!

Another variation you might like to try is using butterscotch or chocolate pudding (with vanilla chips or marshmallows stirred in for the termites) in place of the tapioca.

▶ **Try This**

Like a Hole in the Head

Look through a paper towel roll or toilet paper roll by holding it up to your right eye. With both eyes open and looking straight ahead, place your left hand up against the tube with the palm facing you. Keep staring straight ahead. Do you see the hole in your hand?

Good Bug, Bad Bug

Bad bugs like the striped cucumber beetle can cause a lot of damage in your garden. But another beetle, the familiar spotted ladybug, is a very good bug to have around your plants! Find your way through this garden by making a path that alternates bad bug and good bug. You can move up and down or side to side, but not diagonally. If your path comes to a "No Bugs" sign, you're going in the wrong direction—try again!

Farming Pests

Now, it's time to leave the comforts of your home and travel to the countryside. Have you ever visited a farm? Let's say you are a farmer. You till the land, plant your seeds, and then hope for sunshine and rain. Nothing to it, really, right? Well, not exactly. Once you've finished planting, you need to take care of the small plants that sprout from the ground—they need your protection from weeds and, of course, from hungry bugs!

And you'd be surprised what a menace these bugs can be. Bugs like the grasshopper will eat everything in their path. Sure, a few bugs can't eat very much. But once they invite all their bug friends to share the crops, watch out—hundreds of bugs can consume an entire field of corn or beans and many other types of crops.

Because insects may destroy crops, one natural way of dealing with them is crop rotation. Here is how it works: You switch what you grow on a particular field from year to year. Let's say you grow soybeans, and bugs that just love soybeans come and live in your field. Next year, if you plant soybeans again, there'll be even more of those bugs, and your crop would most likely be destroyed. If, however, you switch to growing broccoli next year, those bugs will decide that this kind of food is not for them, and will move on in search of food elsewhere. And by the time those bugs that love broccoli figure out that you've got it right there in your field, it'll be almost time for the harvest.

On the Path of Destruction

Every year thousands of dollars of crops are devastated or destroyed by insects. To prevent this type of damage, scientists try to produce seeds that are resistant to these bugs. Despite potential losses, farmers must leave one-fifth of all of their crops untreated as a refuge for the insects to survive in, to prevent their possible total extinction.

Grass Hopping

Grasshoppers, which are also known as *locusts*, can jump a distance of up to twenty times their own length. How far can you and your team jump? Hold a Grasshopper Jump competition by having the first person in each line jump as far as they

can. The second person starts their jump where the first person left off. The winning team is the team with the longest total distance jumped.

WORDS to KNOW

resistant crops: Crops that can withstand or repel disease or pests (such as insects). Crops may be treated with chemicals or have their genetic makeup altered to provide different kinds of resistance.

Corn Creamers

Here's how bugs can destroy a whole field of corn. When the corn plants first start to grow, they are invaded by billbugs, which drill holes in the corn stalks. Then, the European corn borers take over. Starting with the whorl, corn borers move down into the center of the plant, eating through the base of the stalks and finally getting to the corn ears. And when they finish their meals, leaving nothing but destroyed corn plants behind them, the corn borers emerge as full-grown moths, ready to lay eggs for the next year's generation.

A caterpillar crawled across the counter of a fast-food restaurant and ordered a thick shake. It quickly drank the whole shake, crawled back across the counter, and left the restaurant.

"That's amazing!" a customer said to the clerk behind the counter.

"You're right," replied the clerk. "He usually orders large fries."

The Mystery of Crop Circles

Even if you find a way to trick those bugs and prevent them from eating your crops, you may not be able to save your field from destruction caused by crop circles. Several farmers have claimed that they are victims of this weird phenomenon.

A crop circle is formed when someone or something (and who knows who or what that may be) bends stalks of wheat, corn, or other crops to the ground in patterns that appear like drawings if you were to look at the field from above. They are usually circular, which is why they are called "crop circles." The damage looks nothing like grasshopper holes, ear-worm bites, or even corn-borer devastation.

If you visit a Web site that talks about crop circles, you can see how the world has been a canvas for this type of art—according to some sources, crop circles have been around for the past three centuries.

What would you do if the world were your canvas? What would you draw? Go outside and see if you can draw on the ground (or, if you find an empty parking lot, use sidewalk chalk to draw on the asphalt). What do you think your pictures will look like from above?

Some people believe that crop circles are formed by heat. Heating corn can change it into different forms—that's how you can make popcorn, for instance. Speaking of different forms, do you think bugs know about these five different types of corn? They are:

- **Grain corn:** used as animal feed and for making corn flake cereal.
- **Sweet corn:** what we eat on the cob, or out of the can, with butter on it.
- **Popcorn:** sold for popping and eating.
- **Seed corn:** used for planting crops each year.
- **Ornamental corn:** brightly colored corn that is used for decoration.

Why was the gardener jumping up and down?
He had ants in his pants!

How does a kernel of corn get turned into popcorn? Well, as the kernel is heated, the water inside it turns into steam and causes the kernel to burst open, turning itself inside out. The white fluffy stuff is the starch that has been "cooked" in the popcorn popper.

So, next time you are watching a movie at home, how about making some popcorn? You can leave it unflavored, or add butter, salt, or sprinkled cheese. If your family likes caramel popcorn, your parents can warm half a cup of margarine and a cup of sugar over medium heat, stirring the mixture constantly, until it is caramel-colored, and then pour the very hot syrup over the bowl of popcorn and stir. You can eat it when it cools.

Hole-y Sweater!

Oh, dear! Your good woolen sweater has been chewed to bits by some kind of bug! Use a pencil to shade in the squares that are listed. When you're finished, you will have a picture of the critter that invaded your closet.

Column 1: C, D
Column 2: B, C, D, E, F, M, N, O, P, Q
Column 3: B, D, F, L, M, O, Q
Column 4: B, D, F, G, K, L, M, O, Q
Column 5: C, D, F, G, J, K, M, N, O, Q
Column 6: C, D, F, H, J, K, M, P, Q
Column 7: A, E, F, H, J, K, L, M, N, O, P
Column 8: B, D, G, H, J, K
Column 9: C, D, E, G, H, I, J, K, L, M
Column 10: F, G, H, I, J, K, L, M, N
Column 11: C, D, E, G, H, I, J, K, L, M
Column 12: B, D, G, H, J, K
Column 13: A, E, F, H, J, K, L, M, N, O, P
Column 14: C, D, F, H, J, K, M, P, Q
Column 15: C, D, F, G, J, K, M, N, O, Q
Column 16: B, D, F, G, K, L, M, O, Q
Column 17: B, D, F, L, M, O, Q
Column 18: B, C, D, E, F, M, N, O, P, Q
Column 19: C, D

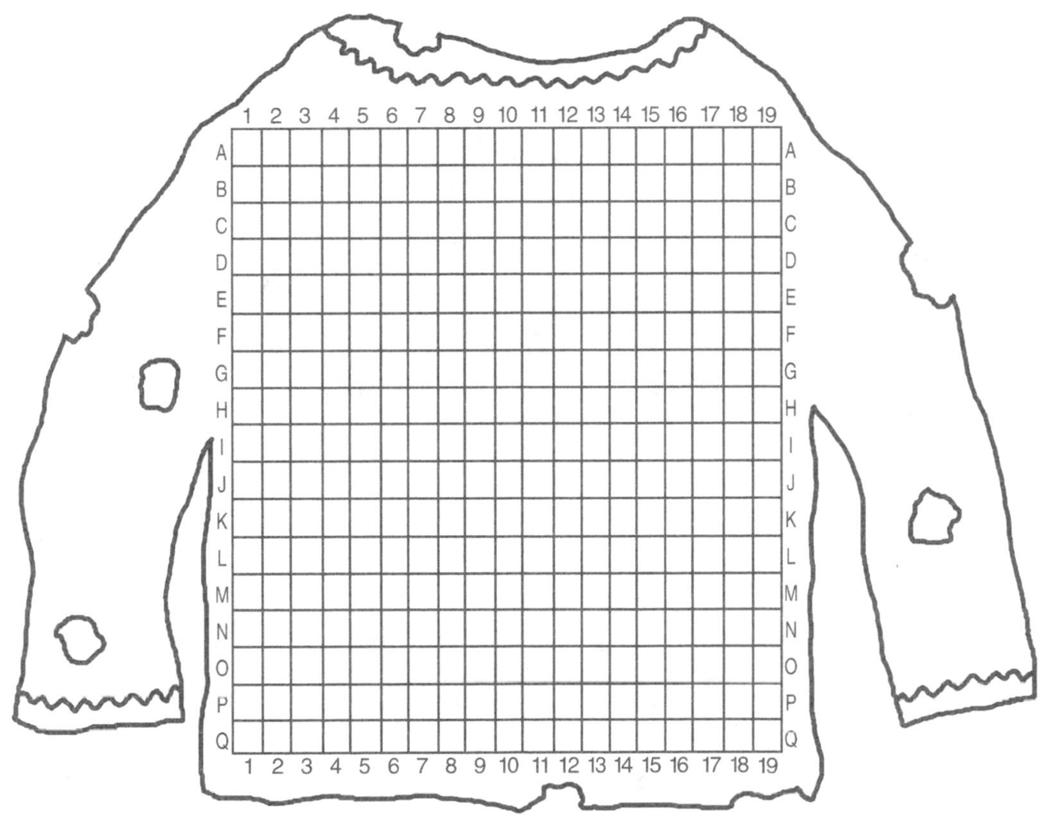

Moths and Cloths

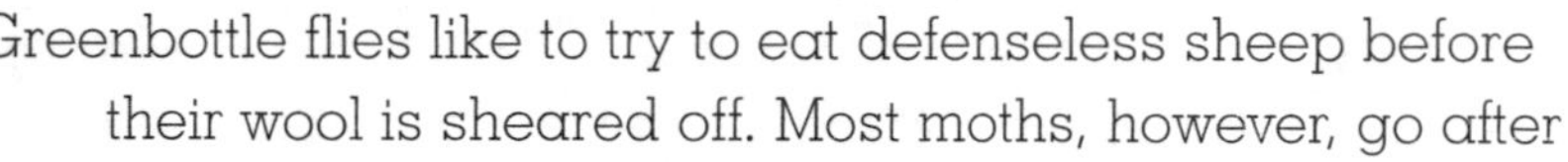

Greenbottle flies like to try to eat defenseless sheep before their wool is sheared off. Most moths, however, go after wool after it's made into your favorite sweater. Maybe these moths are just dizzy from all that circling. What other reason could they have for eating someone else's hair? They've never told us, but keep your woolen sweaters, scarves, and mittens far, far away from them!

We get our wool from sheep. First, the sheep gets a haircut and the sheared wool is cleaned (any bugs that live in the warm, dense wool must bid their home goodbye). Then the wool is dyed and carded or brushed flat, into a sliver. The slivers are rolled into a cord, or yarn, and eventually weaved into cloth or knitted into a sweater. Apparently, moths think that all this work is done just so they can have a nice pretty sweater for dinner. To protect your clothes from moths, place some cedar chips or a few mothballs in your closet. Moths can't stand that stuff.

FUN FACT

Why Wool Is Warm

Why do we make our warmest clothes out of wool? Because it works like an insulator: it keeps your body heat inside your clothes and does not allow it to escape. But did you also know that wool keeps the heat out too? The principle is the same; it does not allow heat to cross through, whether inside or out.

Going to the Moon

Moths are known by the "circling" patterns they make as they fly, but the only time they do so is when we can see them. Most of the time they fly in a straight line, guided by the light of the moon. However, when they see our lights, they get confused by these impostor moons, and try to switch course, which causes them to fly in circles. You can try to confuse moths even further by flashing two flashlights on and off, one at a time. If you succeed in tricking the poor moth, you'll see it flying back and forth from one flashlight to the other.

Chapter 5

Growing Bugs

Butterfly Gardens

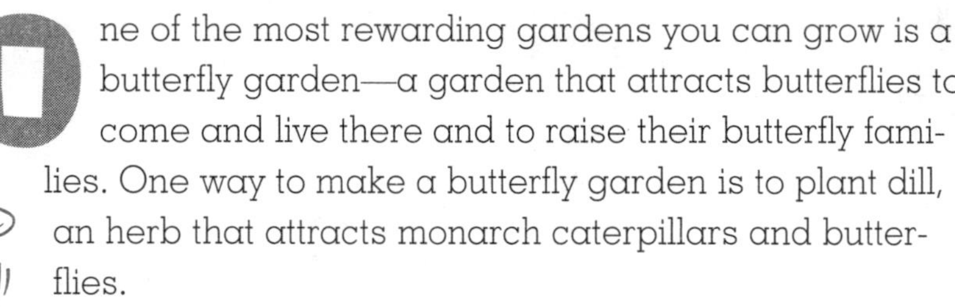

One of the most rewarding gardens you can grow is a butterfly garden—a garden that attracts butterflies to come and live there and to raise their butterfly families. One way to make a butterfly garden is to plant dill, an herb that attracts monarch caterpillars and butterflies.

When the mother monarch butterfly finds good-tasting dill plants, she will lay her eggs there. When the little caterpillars hatch from the eggs, they'll have plenty of food to eat as they grow to eventually become adult butterflies. Another plant that will attract monarchs is the milkweed, which sets a good background for butterfly breeding.

Here's a list of some other things to plant and which bugs like it:

cabbage	cabbage butterfly
clover	the wooly bear caterpillar; tiger moth
parsley	black swallowtail
dogwood	common blue butterfly
trumpet vine	plebeian sphinx moth
cosmos	hummingbird moth
larkspur	all different types of butterflies

breeding: When two insects mate for the purpose of reproduction (producing offspring). Breeding can bring change as two different parents create a new type of baby bug.

Many of the flowers that you plant for the butterflies will also attract moths. And although they seem a lot alike, they are different in four ways:

1. Butterflies hold their wings together while at rest; moths lay them flat.
2. Butterfly antennae have bumps on the ends; moth antennae are thick and feathery.

3. Butterflies prefer the daytime; moths come out at night.
4. Butterfly bodies are thin; moth bodies are usually thick.

Party Time!

Dips are good to eat with chips, raw vegetables, or crackers. Or you can spread them over a bagel or croissant and add thin veggies and cheese to make veggie pizza. Dips are great for parties too—you can serve Dilly Dip at your next butterfly-garden party!

Dilly Dip

If you're curious what a monarch caterpillar sees in the dill, try tasting it yourself. Fresh dill is sometimes available at the vegetable section of the grocery store; if not, you can buy dried dill in the spice section. One great way to eat dill is by making dill dip.

If you'd like to make your very own Dilly Dip, all you need to do is combine the following ingredients:

- 1 cup **sour cream**
- 1 teaspoon of **dried dill** (finely diced)
- ½ teaspoon of **onion powder**
- A dash of **seasoning salt**

Or try adding any of these for a new taste sensation: cream cheese, olives, sandwich spread, or pineapple.

What stroke does a caterpillar use when it swims?

The butterfly!

Ladybug Gardens

Flower gardeners also like to have ladybugs in their gardens. Why? Because these pretty bugs will eat aphids, which are a menace to the flowers. Another bug that can protect the flowers from pests is the praying mantis. Gardeners can order them too, through a nursery, seed catalog, or over the Internet. Praying mantises will eat most of the crop-damaging insects and keep your garden fairly bug-free. As a matter of fact, if a praying mantis gets hungry enough, it will also eat its own babies and spouse! Female praying mantises have been known to eat the head right off their men!

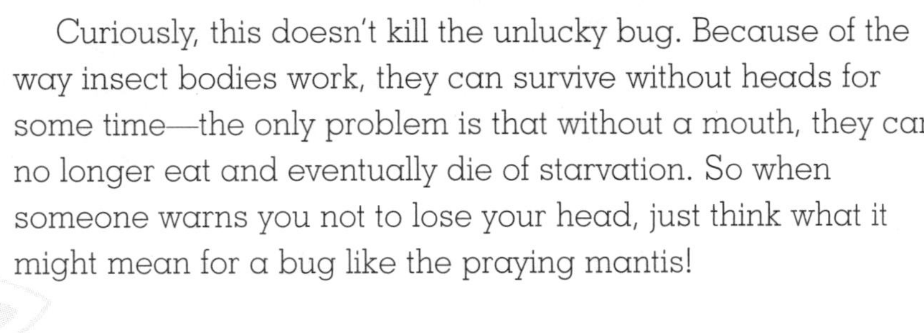

Curiously, this doesn't kill the unlucky bug. Because of the way insect bodies work, they can survive without heads for some time—the only problem is that without a mouth, they can no longer eat and eventually die of starvation. So when someone warns you not to lose your head, just think what it might mean for a bug like the praying mantis!

Amazing Butterfly Facts

Butterflies can taste with their feet and they can hear and smell with their antennae. A butterfly cannot harm anything because it is unable to bite or chew. It only has a tongue called a "proboscis" that curls and uncurls like a party blower to sip nectar. The name "butterfly" means "scale wing."

A butterfly's feathery scales come in all shapes and colors. The combination of veins and scales make the butterfly able to fly and glide. In fact, we learned a lot from these creatures. Can you guess which insect may have inspired these inventions?

- gliders
- tunnels
- helicopters
- hammocks
- flashlights
- tents
- needles
- nets
- camouflage
- straws
- apartment houses

There is another reason why butterfly wings are special. Whether you are looking at the smallest butterfly (a dwarf blue), which is ½ inch in size, or the gigantic white birdwing butterfly (over 12 inches tall), every one is different. The patterns on the butterfly wings are as individual and unique as snowflakes—there are no two that are exactly alike.

Who Am I?

I am one of the few insects that molt (or shed my skin) five times. My small size (a mere ¼ inch!) makes it very easy for me to hide inside crevices and cracks. I hunt for food at night where you lay your head. **Who am I?**

(A bed bug)

▶ Try This

On the Lookout for Butterflies

Another place to look for butterflies is in shrubs and trees where they often will go to form their chrysalis (the case that holds them as a pupa). Butterflies also like to gather near mud holes to drink and to dance. When the weather is bad, these delicate bugs take cover in the leaves of nearby trees or flowers.

To examine the little butterfly wings, you will need a microscope or a magnifying glass. If you don't have either one of these, how about making your own magnifying tool? It's actually very easy. What you need is a clear plastic egg or trinket holder (the kind that comes out of a toy machine) or a clear plastic soft drink bottle. If you pour a little water into the bottom of one of these and then hold it over a bug or some of the words in this book, you will see them better.

What insect walks like this—99, thump, 99, thump, 99, thump?

A centipede with a wooden leg!

Potato Bugs

The potato bug, also known as the Colorado beetle, is a small beetle decorated with vertical stripes—nothing to be afraid of, right? Well, did you know that no one can scare potato farmers as much as the potato bug? That's because a few of these bugs can easily ruin an entire potato crop.

This wasn't always the case. A long, long time ago, potatoes didn't really grow in North America, and the potato bug was nowhere to be seen either. The first people to cultivate (grow) potatoes were the Incas, who lived in South America. When the

Who Am I?

I am a famous for playing "follow the leader." A man named Jean Henri Fabre first discovered my head-to-tail trails on an evergreen tree. If you put me on a bowl with several of my friends, we will follow each other around forever, or at least until we wear down. **Who am I?**

(A Fabre caterpillar)

Europeans arrived to the New World, they tried eating potatoes, liked them, and took them back to Europe with them, where they became very popular. In fact, when the first immigrants came to North America, they brought the potato plants with them. Now that's a journey to be proud of!

And what about the potato bugs? Well, they weren't always known for their love of potatoes. Originally from Mexico, these pesky bugs survived on a plant known as buffalo bur. As the potatoes were introduced throughout North America, the potato bugs got a taste as well, and they liked them so much that they gave up the buffalo bur for good!

One of the reasons the potato bug has become such an enemy to the potato farmer is due to its ability to develop so quickly. The eggs, which quickly change to larvae, feed for just three weeks then drop into the ground, returning ten days later as adult beetles ready to lay eggs. The only thing slowing these beetles down is they have a few enemies of their own, such as toads, snakes, ladybird beetles, birds, wasps, flies, and stinkbugs, to name a few.

▶ Try This

Lines and Stripes

Draw two outlines of a beetle. On one, add vertical stripes; on the other, make the stripes horizontal. Which beetle appears larger? Now, take two more outlines and color one beetle a light color and the other one dark. Is there any difference in how they appear? Now, consider this: If you're trying to look taller, which way should you wear your stripes? And if you want your room to look bigger, what shades of paint should you choose?

Crawly Clues

You often find bugs hiding in the objects around you. What would it be like if you found everyday objects hiding in the bugs instead? Look carefully at the name of each bug. Find and circle the letters, reading from left to right, that spell out the answer to each clue. Write the answer on the line provided. The first one is done for you.

1. Cinderella's carriage COACH COCKROACH
2. Colorful subject in school ______ TARANTULA
3. Tasty dessert ______ SPIDER
4. Type of medicine ______ CATERPILLAR
5. Things worn on fingers ______ PRAYING MANTIS
6. Red vegetable ______ BEETLE
7. Between shoulder and hand ______ EARTHWORM
8. Move your hand back and forth ______ GRUB
9. Grain served steamed or boiled ______ CRICKET
10. Place to buy things ______ GRASSHOPPER
11. Man's neckwear ______ TERMITE
12. Vegetable on a cob ______ SCORPION
13. Sturdy work boat ______ STINK BUG

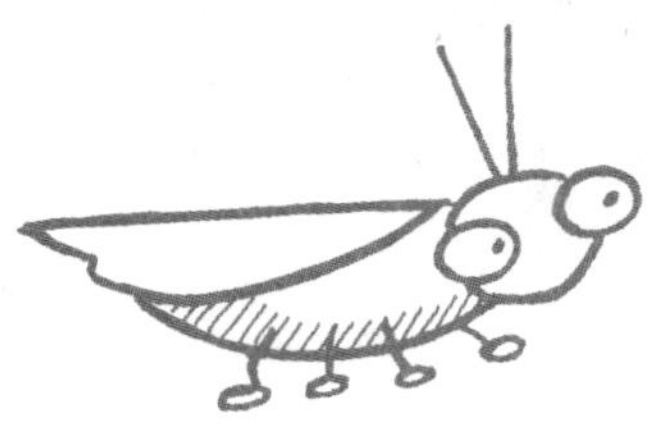

Another bug that is very fond of potatoes is the June bug grub—it especially loves the potato roots. In fact, this grub will stay underground for two years before deciding to come out in May or June. You may have seen one of these large brown beetles, which come out at night and fly toward the light. If you look closely at a June bug, you will see its antennae are shaped like little antlers.

Dinner Is Served!

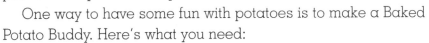

No one could argue with a potato bug, potatoes do taste great. Whether it's potato chips or French fries, baked potatoes or hash browns, almost everyone eats them. Did you know that the average person eats 140 pounds of "spuds" each year?

One way to have some fun with potatoes is to make a Baked Potato Buddy. Here's what you need:

- A few **potatoes** (one per person), baked and cooled
- Several **toothpicks**
- **Vegetables** such as carrots, broccoli, olives, and cherry tomatoes and other foods to use as decoration

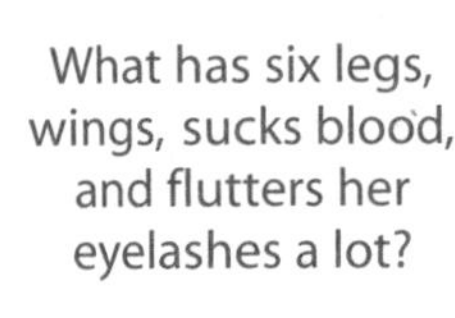

What has six legs, wings, sucks blood, and flutters her eyelashes a lot?
A Miss-quito!

Once you've got all the ingredients together, you can use toothpicks to decorate the potato with the vegetables—for example, make a carrot nose, broccoli hair, olive eyes, or a cherry tomato nose.

If you are making a baked potato bug, you can add tortilla wings (you can even paint them with food coloring by using cotton swabs) and legs that could be made out of pretzels. Maybe the mouth could be part of a green pepper ring or a stinger made from a "bugle" type of chip. The possibilities are endless!

Once you've finished your creation, you can microwave it until it's done. Then remove the toothpicks and add butter and salt to taste. Or you can take your new friend for a "dip" in your Dilly Dip (see page 49).

Another twist on the same idea is to make a squashed bug. If you're having company over, your guests can make their own creations and squash them themselves. Using a precooked squash or potato, add the garnishes: tomatoes for the abdomen, scallions for the antennae, olives or black beans for eyes, cheese spread and bacon bits for the insides, and shaved ham or turkey for the wings. Now all you have to do is bake it for a couple of minutes (you should probably cover it) and then squash it—and it's ready to serve.

With all these food options, you can host an entire spud party for your family and friends. Other menu ideas are potato chips, French fries, hash browns, and a baked potato bar complete with cheese, ketchup, sour cream, dip, chili, and more.

FUN FACT

It's French to Me

The French did not really invent French fries. People in England, Belgium, and other countries have long known how to make fried potatoes. So why do we call them French? According to one popular theory, American soldiers during World War I ate a lot of fries in France. When, they came home, they referred to them as French fries, and the name stuck.

Bug's Eye View

Everything looks different when you are as small as a bug. To a bug, a coffee cup looks as big as an office building! Try and figure out what each of these simple pictures represents from the viewpoint of a bug—match them with the list below. **Remember, think small!**

Head of a pin
Edge of a pencil
Looking out of a soda can
Hair on your arm
Edge of a dime
Grain of salt

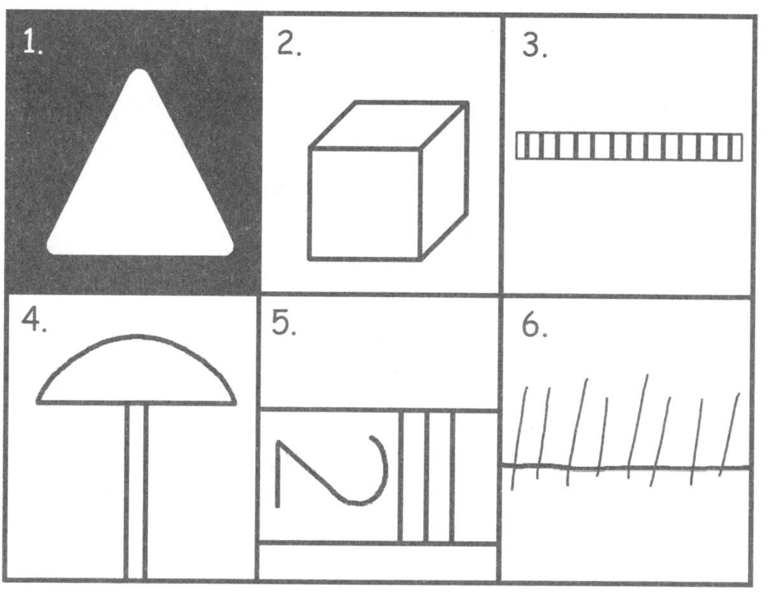

Growing Potatoes

Now it's your turn to grow potatoes. Take two raw potatoes—one plain brown potato and one sweet potato—and put each one into a glass jar filled with water, so that only a half of each potato is covered with water. Now, set the two jars on a sunny windowsill, and see what happens. You should get results within the next two weeks.

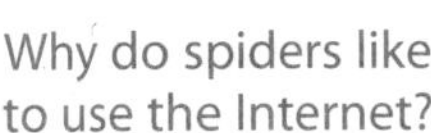

Why do spiders like to use the Internet?

They love to check out the Web sites!

Farming Ants

Did you know that ants are farmers? They farm leaves, grow fungus, and even milk aphids. Milking an aphid may sound sort of hard to do, but for an ant it's fairly simple. When an ant strokes the aphid with its feelers, the aphid releases a sweet honeydew that the ant collects for food—just like dairy farmers collect milk from cows. Most ant farmers work around the clock to care for their colony.

The ant colony is a tightly run community led by the queen, whose job it is to lay all the ant eggs. The rest of the colony includes worker ants, nursery ants, and soldier ants, which all happen to be female. Occasionally, some eggs hatch into male ants, which mate with the queen and die shortly after. (The other ants do live long lives: workers live about seven years and queens can live up to fifteen years.)

Many ant colonies live in anthills, which you may find in forested areas. Underneath each anthill is a large nest, its own little world that is rarely disturbed. When something does happen, restoring and repairing the nest is the ants' number-one priorit

colony: In the world of bugs, this is a group of animals or insects (like ants, for instance) that live and work together.

Edible Ant Hills

One treat you can cook is called an Edible Anthill. You will need parental participation for this one, as it requires the use of a stove. Here's what you need before you get started:

- 1 cup of **sugar**
- 1 cup of **corn syrup**
- 1 cup of **peanut butter**
- 1 teaspoon of **vanilla**
- 6 cups of **O-shaped oat cereal**
- **Chocolate chips and raisins**, to taste

Combine the sugar (an ant's favorite thing) and corn syrup in a pan and bring them to a boil. As soon as the mixture boils, remove the pan from heat and add peanut butter and vanilla. Then, stir in the cereal and spoon the mixture into several mounds on a buttered cookie sheet or waxed paper. When cool enough to touch, add chocolate chips or raisin "ants" to your mounds, and your anthills are ready to be served. These will keep well in the refrigerator or in a sealed container—if they aren't eaten up first!

Diversity in the Ant World

There are 2,500 different kinds of ants; some of the more famous ones are the fire ant, the army ant, and the honeypot ant. The fire ant gets its name from its terrible burning sting that is as painful to a human as a sting of a wasp or a bee. The army ant marches like the soldiers of a real army. They also fight and hunt for prey. The honeypot ant serves the purpose of storage in its colony—its abdomen is the pot that stores honey. When the honeypot ant's abdomen is filled with honey, it can reach the size of a cherry. Unable to move from the great weight, the ant just hangs there, from the roof of the nest, feeding the other ants in times of need.

▶ Try This

Amazing Maze

If you want to test ant skills, build a small maze with six to ten turns and see how long it takes for an ant to find a sugar cube at the end of the maze. You can make your maze out of wooden Popsicle sticks and some glue.

Build an Ant Farm

What has six legs, wings, sucks blood, and uses a code with dots and dashes?

A morse-quito!

Ants are fascinating creatures that you can watch for hours. And you can do just that if you have an ant farm with glass sides that will allow you a glimpse into the ant world. To construct one yourself, you can use two wide-mouthed jars, one larger than the other.

First, you place the smaller jar inside the larger one. Then you fill the space between the jars with a few cups of ant-filled dirt from outside (with workers, eggs, larvae, and a queen, if possible). You will want to cover the top of the largest jar with a piece of cloth and use a rubber band to hold it in place. When it's finished, it's best to place your ant farm in a pan of water, just in case an ant should escape through the cloth. Ants can't swim, so they will stay inside your "moat"-surrounded farm as long as there is enough water to hold them in there.

You can feed, water, and study these ants for a small period of time and then return them to the place where you found them. Ants like breadcrumbs soaked in sugar water and dead flies or bugs. You can also add bread soaked in plain water for them to drink. Too much water can drown them or destroy their nest, so take care in adding just the right amount for them. Your farm should see some sun, but not direct light for any period of time, as it could bake the ants.

The Power of Communication

Ants have a very advanced communication system—they can talk to each other and give directions to where the food is, and they are also able to learn from their experiences.

To see this higher-level thinking in action, all you have to do is have a picnic. Before long, these bugs will be joining you for a free lunch. And if you're not careful, they'll haul most of it off while you're not looking. Time to run and hide? Just try moving the picnic over a few feet. Still, before long they'll figure it out.

Many people believe insects can't really think—they are just following their natural instincts. All living creatures have natural instincts, including you. A few common instincts are:

- Respecting or fearing **water**.
- Looking for **food**.
- Finding **shelter** in a storm.
- Knowing when you're about to get in **trouble**.

Scavenging for Food

Ants look for food with the help of their antennae, which they use to smell. Sounds easy? Why not try it for yourself? Here is how you can have an ant treasure hunt.

Wear a blindfold as you hunt for a strong-smelling food like fresh-baked cookies or fresh strawberries. (Of course, you will need a person who is not blindfolded to hide the food and then help you move around as you search for it.)

communication: One way an animal or insect gives a message to another. Ants communicate or "talk" by touching their antennae. Through this touch, an ant can tell the rest of the colony where the food is.

FUN FACT

Fooled Ya!

There are only two times when ants don't seem all that bright. One, when they bring the caterpillar of the large blue butterfly into their nest. The ants want to taste the sweet fluid it releases, but all the caterpillar wants is to eat the ant's larva. Two, when a colony is tricked by a "cuckoo" queen and her workers, who take over another queen's nest.

The Ants Go Marching One by One

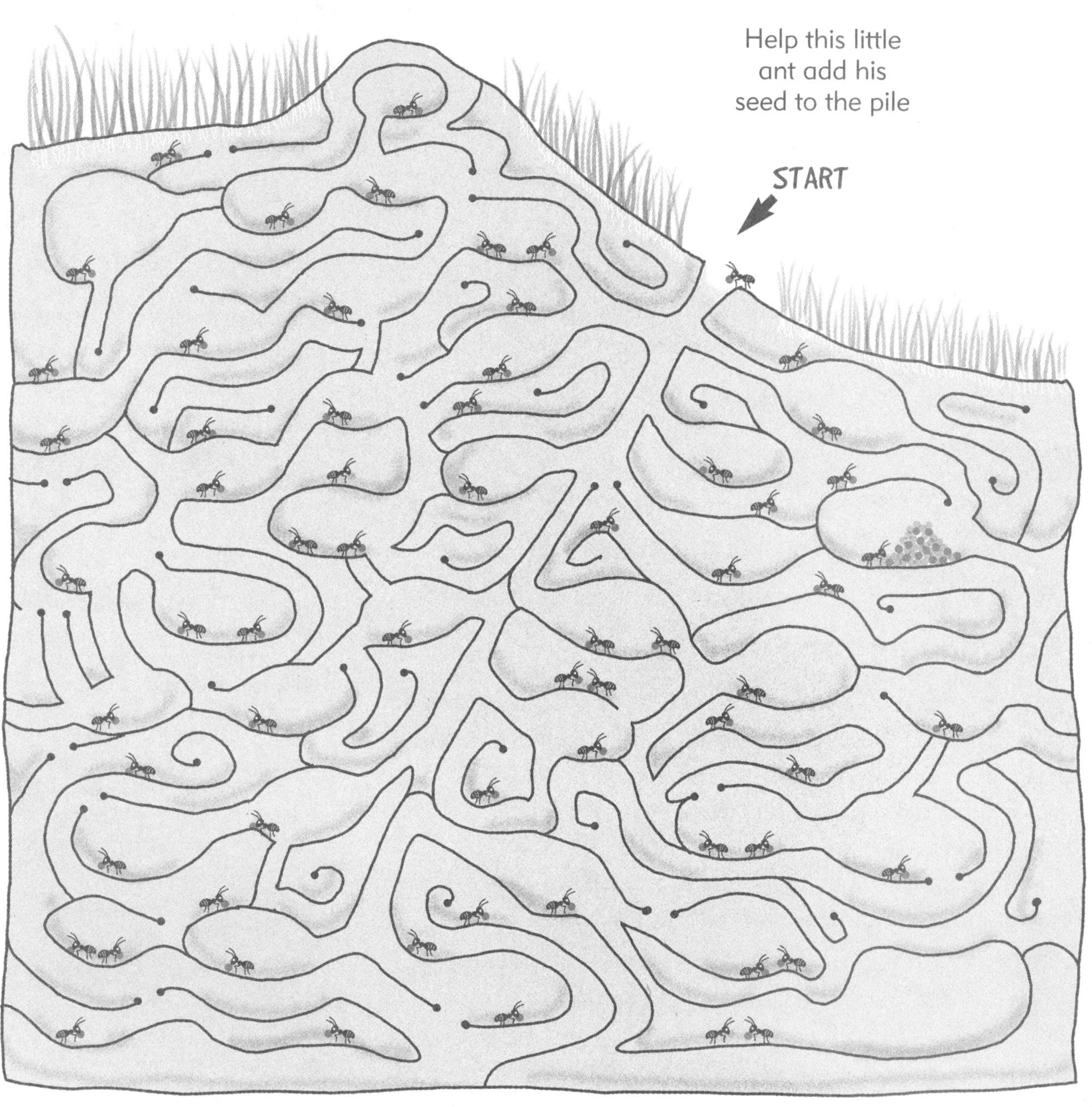
Help this little ant add his seed to the pile
START

Chapter 6

Bugs Underground

Digging Around

A "dig" is another word for an excavation. Treasure hunters, archaeologists, and miners who look for gold, silver, and diamonds underground all dig for treasure—and so can you, with the help of an adult. Grownups can come in handy for finding safe places to dig. There are more than just bugs underground. Phone lines, gas lines, cable connections, and water pipes are also found there, and they can be dangerous. They're not all that far down underneath, either, so be careful! A garden (where someone digs regularly) would probably be the best spot to start with.

Once you find the perfect spot, dig in. Taking a spade or shovel, scoop some of the ground up and spread it out on a piece of cardboard or a tarp. What do you see? You'll be amazed at how many insects you can find in one shovelful of dirt.

Now, you can separate all the bugs into groups:

- **Apterygota:** Insects with no wings, like bristletails and springtails.
- **Endopterygota:** Insects that go through many changes as they grow—flies, butterflies, beetles, ants, and many others that you are likely familiar with.
- **Exopterygota:** Insects that do not change very much as they grow. This group includes termites, lice, dragonflies, and other bugs.

Endopterygota usually go through the following four stages: egg, larval (or caterpillar), pupal, and adult (for example, an adult butterfly).

Some of the creatures you find underground may not look like bugs at all. Some may be eggs or grubs. Or they may be nymphs, like that of the cicada. If you look on the bark of a tree

How do hopping bugs start a race?
"One, two, flea, GO!"

WORDS to KNOW

anthropod: A joint-legged creature. All insects are anthropods, but not all anthropods are insects. Some are just close relatives, like the spider and the centipede. One way to know whether something is an insect is to remember that insects have six legs when they are fully grown.

in the months of July and August, you may find a nymph that has already climbed up out of the ground or one that has climbed completely out of its shell.

grub: The larvae of some insects before they are fully grown. Many grubs have a wormlike shape to them.

A Treasure in Your Own Garden

When you looked through your shovel of dirt did you see any money or other treasures? For fun, why not bury your own treasure? Just seal it in a container, hide it in the ground, and draw a treasure map that will lead someone lucky enough to figure it out to the treasure. Then, invite some of your friends over and let the treasure hunt begin!

Or, you can hold a scavenger hunt to see who can find the most items from the list below (you can give yourself unlimited time or set a time limit of ten or twenty minutes). All you need to start the hunt is a jar to collect all your treasures:

- 2 black **ants**
- 1 cicada **shell**
- A **leaf** that looks like someone has been munching on it
- 1 **beetle** (any kind will do)
- 3 **rocks**
- A piece of **tree bark**
- **Something that flies** but doesn't sting

What do you think would be a good prize for the person who wins the scavenger hunt? How about an insect-identification guide? You can make it yourself—all you need is an encyclopedia that contains information about insects or access to the World Wide Web. Learn about different insects, and compile the information in a journal—and you've got the perfect prize (although after all that hard work, you just might want to keep it for yourself).

Who Am I?

One of my favorite hiding places is in a book. You may have seen me somewhere between the pages or in the covers. I like to eat mold and other things like cereal. My last name rhymes with "house." **Who am I?**

(A book louse)

Superb Digging Techniques

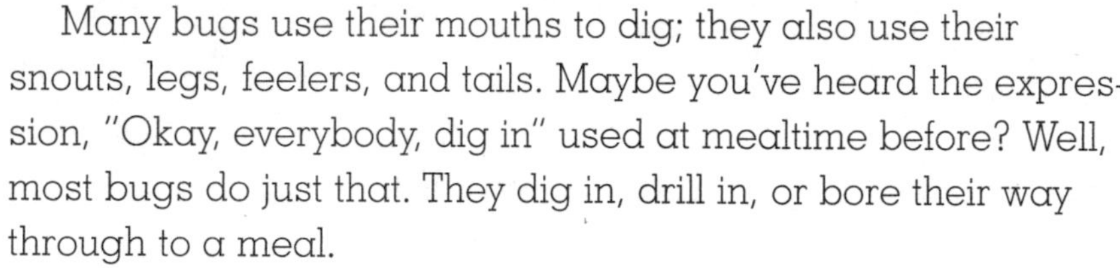

Many bugs use their mouths to dig; they also use their snouts, legs, feelers, and tails. Maybe you've heard the expression, "Okay, everybody, dig in" used at mealtime before? Well, most bugs do just that. They dig in, drill in, or bore their way through to a meal.

A mother acorn weevil makes a reservation for her babies' dinner in advance. First, she drills a hole into the acorn, and then she drops her babies down inside. If you find an acorn in the fall with a small hole in it, there may be weevils for you to see in the spring. Leave the acorn outside throughout the winter, then gently open it in the early spring. The weevil you are looking for will have a really long snout.

Where's the Bug?

Circle or underline the name of the bug hidden in each sentence. Names can be found in either the middle of a word, or by combining the end of one word with the beginning of the next.

1. My mother bakes the best cookies.
2. It was Peter's idea to play cards.
3. James was a giant peach for Halloween.
4. Why is a cap hidden under the bed?
5. There's always one beet left over!
6. I need a long rubber band.
7. I'll have a waffle after I finish my juice.

▶ Try This

The Art of Mud

Another muddy mess you can get yourself into is mud painting. With your family's permission you can take some real mud, water it down, and paint the walks or driveway using an old paintbrush. Once you've had your fun with mud, don't forget to clean up. Using a garden hose, soak down your paintings and then sweep them away with a broom.

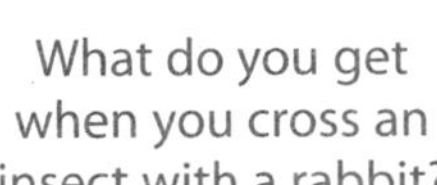

What do you get
when you cross an
insect with a rabbit?
Bugs Bunny!

Dirt, Grime, and Mud

Have you ever played a joke on someone? Well, this joke is sort of a "dirty" one. If you want to gross out your friends, invite them to your house and ask them if they realize that some people actually eat bugs and dirt. Then, take a spoon out of your pocket and scoop up some dirt from a nearby potted plant and eat it!

Gross, huh? Well, actually, it's only a trick! The plant is actually made of silk and the dirt is really crunched-up graham crackers and chocolate cookies mixed together in a clean pot. Once your friends figure out what's going on, you can share the treat with them.

Here is another way to get down and dirty in mud—make mud pies. Mix your edible crackers-and-cookies soil with pudding and whipped cream, or use it as topping on your favorite ice cream.

Playing with mud has no limits. You can use your chocolate-pudding mud to finger-paint on cookie sheets or waxed paper. Or you can use an icing bag (the kind your parents might have for decorating cakes) to muddy up your pie with all kinds of decorations and designs.

Who Am I?

My very shiny body is a warning not to eat me. Those who ignore the warning and get my blood on them will soon have the blisters to prove it. I belong to the beetle family. Flowers are my favorite food. **Who am I?**

(A blister beetle)

▶ Try This

Let's Play Dung Ball!

If you haven't shocked or amazed your friends enough already, how about inviting them to play a round of dung ball? To play, all you need are several big rubber balls. The object of the game is to roll your ball using only your feet, which is how a real dung beetle does it; the first to the finish line is the winner. For a few variations, try pushing the ball with only your head, your knee, or your heel (going backwards).

Eggs for Safekeeping

Many insects lay eggs, which then hatch into fully grown bugs or into grubs. Often, these eggs need time to hatch and many insects hide them by burying them in the ground. Other insect parents lay the eggs on carcasses of dead animals; still others are laid in an animal that's still living. The dung beetle (also known as a *scarab beetle*) has its own interesting approach to laying eggs. For thousands of years, these beetles have been rolling up balls of dung (droppings of other animals) and laying their eggs inside them. When the grubs hatch, they dine on the dung!

What's the best hairdo for a wasp?
A buzz cut!

And yet, despite this behavior, the scarab beetle was considered to be sacred by the ancient Egyptians. According to them, the scarab beetle had the responsibility of rolling around the ball that represented the sun, and so it was worshipped as a god that made the sun rise in the mornings and set at night. You can still see many images of the scarab beetle in the ancient drawings and jewelry of the Egyptians.

An Underground Observatory in a Jar

In Chapter 3, you learned how to re-create a small part of the outside world at home by filling an aquarium with natural objects and bugs you found outside. Now, how about re-creating the world of underground bugs? All you need is a large jar or see-through container with a screen or a lid with holes that you can fill with some dirt.

The best place to find your bugs-filled dirt is in the garden. Many of the grubs or larvae eat the roots or plants that we plant there. Once you have a few cups of garden soil, pour it into the container. Be sure you add a little plant life and water from time to time. Remember: Insects that live in the ground like dark, cool, and damp places. For the time of your observation, you may need to keep your container in a basement or a shady area.

Remember to keep checking on your "soon to be" bugs. If after several days you still haven't seen any changes, add a few more cups of dirt from a new place. A few types of bugs only live where there are leaves or logs. If you lift a log or move a pile of leaves, you may see a devil's coach beetle. Few people have ever seen one, as they come out only at night to eat caterpillars and spiders.

When you see a hole in your yard, it may actually be some insect's front door. Around sunset, most ground-dwelling insects come home. If you watch from a distance, you may see a bumblebee, digger wasp, or hornworm caterpillar.

FUN FACT

Get to Know the Hornworm

A hornworm is actually a sphinx moth in caterpillar's clothing. Its favorite food is the leaves of a tomato plant. Special hormones tell the caterpillar when it's time to stop eating and to start digging its way underground to form a pupa. If you look closely at its back, you can see a long green throbbing line. This is the hornworm's heart.

Illusions and Camouflage

Bugs disguise themselves every day. Sometimes it's necessary for survival and sometimes it's for hunting purposes. Many of these insects use illusion to hide from their enemies or to keep them away.

Some of the insects are very good at the game of hide-and-seek:

- The **owl butterfly** looks like an owl with its eyes open wide.
- **Thorn bugs** are easily mistaken for real thorns.
- A **flower mantis** is shaped like a bright pink flower.
- Dead **leaf butterflies** can pass for a dead leaf without any problem.

A lot of insects try to look like something else. A wasp beetle looks like a wasp; predators on the lookout for beetles will avoid the wasp beetle because they are afraid of wasps!

Master of Illusions

Now you see it, now you don't. What are you really seeing? Try this illusion—all you need are scissors and colored paper (make sure you have at least four different colors). Take one piece of paper, and cut out four small circles of the same size. Then, cut out four squares (each should be the same size, and they should be larger than the circles), but this time use a different color for each square. Now, if you place the circles over the squares, can you see what happens? Some circles will appear smaller than others—even though you *know* that they are identical in size. This trick truly shows that things aren't always as they appear.

Mixed-Up Flies

Everybody knows that caterpillars change into butterflies. But did you know that a butterfly can become a firefly? You can do it in four steps if you make the right compound words.

BUTTERFLY to
FLY__________ to
______________ to
______________ to
FIREFLY

Look-alikes

Which butterfly exactly matches the picture from the guidebook?

1.

2.

3.

Itsy-bitsy

A pictograph is a very simple drawing—kind of like visual shorthand. Can you guess what this little pictograph shows?

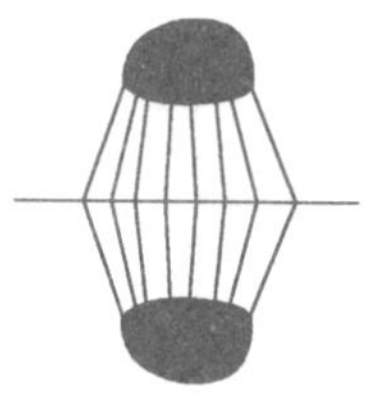

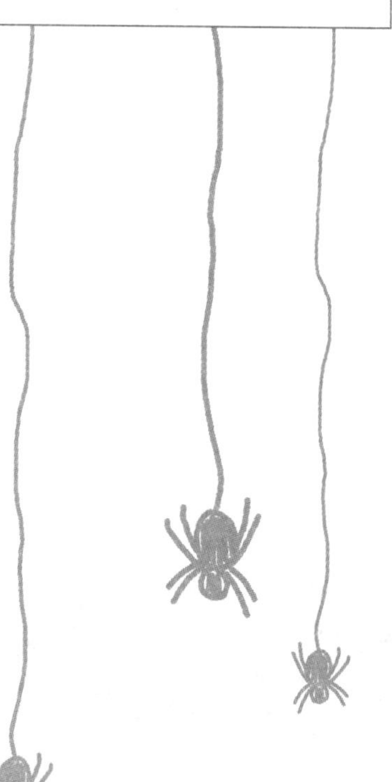

Host a Disguise Party

Nature has given some bugs excellent disguises, and it's not a bad idea for humans to learn from them. Have you ever thought of why army uniforms are patchy green? To blend in with natural surroundings like a field or a forest.

Can you invent disguises that will keep your friends guessing who you are? Hold a disguise party where everyone shows up wearing a disguise, and then hold a contest to see whose disguise works best and who can be recognized. There are lots of great books out there on how to disguise yourself and how to be a detective. Many detectives work in disguise or camouflage to keep the person they are following from knowing who they are.

▶ Try This
Play Hide-and-Seek

Here's a hide-and-seek idea for playing with your bugs. Instead of hiding yourself, why not hide your pet insect or a stuffed-animal bug?

I'm Trapped!

Ever heard of trapdoor spiders? These creatures take disguise to a whole new level—they construct a silk-hinged door that tricks their victims inside their house. The trapdoor opens easily. When a victim approaches, the spider pounces upon it, shooting it with poison. Then, the spider drags the victim down into its burrow and eats it.

The trapdoor spider isn't the only sneaky designer of homes. Tiger beetle larvae will also dig a nice trap in the dirt, where it lays waiting for the next passerby. Similarly, the larvae of the ant lion does the same, but it prefers sand to soil. And if it seems like the wait is taking too long, the impatient ant lion will spit sand at a passing ant and knock it down into the pit.

World Wide (Spider) Web

Spider webs are by far the most famous of all the traps devised by bugs. If you have ever gotten caught trying to walk through a spider web, you know that the silky web strands are sticky and nearly impossible to get off of you. But you are much bigger than the spider web—although you may be annoyed, you can just walk away. But what about a little fly? Once it's trapped, getting away is impossible.

Each type of spider spins a different kind of web. The web-throwing spider builds one of the most amazing spider traps. Once this spider has spun its web, it waits for an unsuspecting bug to pass under it, and then it tosses the net over its victim.

What has eighteen legs and catches flies?

A baseball team!

Some Native Americans weave "dream catcher" types of webs in a circular frame made out of a branch tied into a circle. They use dream catchers to catch bad dreams, while letting the good dreams pass through. Whether you want to make your own dream catcher or a web to catch a ball, it can be a lot of fun and is not difficult.

Making your own web out of rope requires only a few knots and a little weaving. Your web could be circular or square. Both shapes require a frame made of rope. A circular web will need an X-shaped frame; a square web works well with a + shape. You could also weave a web in the fork of a branch, using brightly colored yarn or string.

Speaking of dream catchers and dreams, do you dream in color? It's a question many scientists would like to know the answer to. Some people remember their dreams while others don't. Try keeping track of your dreams. When you wake up in the morning, try to write down what you dreamed about or draw pictures of what you saw in your dreams. Maybe then you'll be able to answer the question about dreaming in color!

Who Am I?

I may look like an ordinary beetle to some, but I am very different in one way. If an enemy tries to attack me, I let out a puff of gas with a very loud bang. If the noise doesn't bother them, the gas will! **Who am I?**

(A bombardier beetle)

What has six legs, wings, sucks blood, and slides on the snow?

A mo-ski-to!

Coming Back to the Surface

If you get tired of digging in the dirt and trying to peel cobwebs off your face, maybe it's time to head back to your room and do some artwork for a change. Drawing insects can be a lot of fun. Bugs' bodies are not all that different from ours. Just like us, they have a head, waist, legs, hair, eyes, mouth—some even have a nose or a snout. However, they do have many body parts that we don't: stingers, antennae, pincers, wings, and a thorax.

First, try to draw bugs as you have seen them in real life or from pictures or photographs that you can find in books or online. You'd be surprised how many details you will notice once you have to draw the entire bug yourself. Then, you can be as creative as you like: Try inventing your own insects or make a drawing of your brother or sister look like a bug.

Feet to Hear

Some insects have come up with entirely different uses for their body parts. For example, a cricket's ears are located on its knees. And flies have special hairs (or sensors) that sprout from their eyes. When they need to clean them, they do it with their feet. What a body-part mishmash!

Have you ever tried using your feet to pick up a spoon or write? Why not try it now? You might be surprised at how much you can do with your feet. What hand do you normally use to write, feed yourself, and brush your teeth? What would happen if you use the other hand? Can you still complete these tasks? Have you ever tried to draw with a pencil using your teeth? Maybe you'll find a talent you never knew you had.

I Luv Bugs

Can you turn these familiar shapes into a fantastic bug? You can add antennae, legs, mouth parts, wings—anything you can think of!

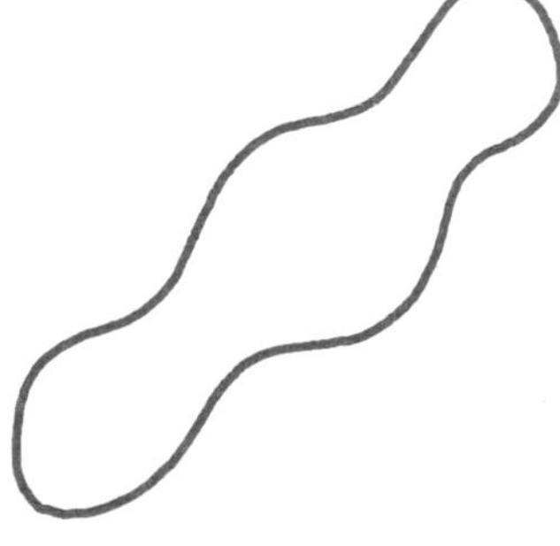

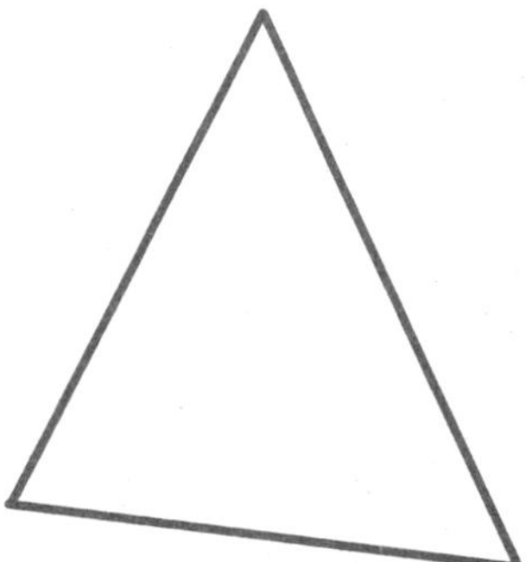

Who Am I?

My name could light up your life, or at least your campground—though most people think that I look like I belong in a swamp. When I'm scared I open my wings and flash two fake eyes at my predators. **Who am I?**

(A lantern bug)

Playing "Hang Bug"

While you have the paper out, how about a game of hang bug? It's just like playing hangman, but instead of hanging a little stick person, you hang a bug from a tree. Here's how it works:

1. Draw a tree for your insect to hang from.
2. Think of a name of a bug that you want the other person to guess.
3. Draw a small line for each letter of the bug's name.

That's when the game begins. You let your friends guess the name of the bug by asking for individual letters. Every time they name a letter that appears in your secret bug's name, you write it in the correct spot. Every time they call out a letter that does not appear in the bug's name, you add another bug body part to the picture: First, you draw the bug's head, then the body, then the six legs, and finally the two antennae. If you complete the picture of the bug before your friends have solved the puzzle, you win!

What is a bug's favorite game?

Tick-tac-toe!

▶ Try This
Sweet 'n' Stinky

You can make your own stink bombs or sweet bombs by filling balloons with vinegar or sugar water. You can launch them somewhere far away from your house and see if any bugs are attracted to the scene. However, don't be a menace! Stink bombs on your friends' clothes or inside the house will *not* be appreciated!

Chapter 7

In Self-Defense

Spitting Ladybugs

How can it be that those cute little ladybugs like to misbehave and spit? Well, maybe they don't really spit—they ooze! And it's very un-ladybug-like, if you think about it. But it's true. Ladybugs (also known as *ladybird bugs*) are one of the friendliest bugs around. So what makes them spit or ooze? Fear. They are afraid of being eaten or harmed and rely on ooze for self-defense. If a bird catches a ladybug for lunch, it just might take a rain check on its meal if the ladybug releases its smelly, bad-tasting ooze from its legs.

If you don't mind being oozed on and want to see how this works, you can do it without harming the ladybug. Just lay it on its back and very gently press on it, *as if* you were going to squeeze it. Once the ladybug realizes that it's in danger, it will ooze right onto your hand. (After you finish this experiment, be sure you wash your hands to get rid of that stinky stuff.)

WORDS to KNOW

self-defense: An animal's way of protecting itself from harm. For example, a wasp will sting not to attack prey, but to protect itself—in self-defense.

Oozing with Fun

You can make many kinds of ooze in imitation of the ladybug. One simple recipe that makes good ooze (even though this one doesn't smell at all) calls for ¾ cup of cornstarch and ½ cup of water. To make it just the right texture, pour the water into a bowl and then slowly add the cornstarch. You can stir this mixture with a spoon or for more fun, with your hands. After mixing the ooze, hold it in your hands. What happens?

This recipe makes 1 cup of ooze, which should be enough for two people to experiment with. If you need more, you can double the recipe. Store your ooze in a plastic container with a lid. If it dries out, just add a little water. To make it more colorful, you can add food coloring, but remember—this ooze is not meant for eating, just to play with!

Spitting Ladybug Cupcakes

If you want to try edible ooze, you can make your own spitting ladybug. First, you'll need a cupcake (any flavor will do). Then, take a stick pretzel and poke six holes about halfway in around the top edge of your cupcake. Mix some instant pudding (this is your edible ooze) by following the directions on the box, and place about half a cup of the pudding in a plastic bag that you can seal. Then, cut the tip off the bottom of the plastic bag and squeeze the pudding into the six holes.

When the holes are filled, stick six pretzels in each one, for the legs. If you want, you can squeeze more ooze into the middle by making a hole in the center of the cupcake with a spoon. Now your cupcake ladybug is ready for her frosting wings and head. The top of the cupcake can be frosted in red or orange. Using a piece of string licorice or another pretzel, put a line across for her head and one down the middle from it, for the wings. For her spots and eyes, you can use any round candy you like. All that's left is to squeeze it and eat it.

Spitting Contests

You don't need to spit in self-defense like the ladybugs do, but you can do it for fun! How about holding a spitting contest? You may be surprised to see just how far your friends and family can actually spit. You may even surprise yourself! All you need is a watermelon and a lot of wide-open space, somewhere outdoors, where it'll be easy to clean up later.

FUN FACT

Ladybug Red

When a ladybug first molts, or sheds, it has no actual color—the bright red color won't appear for a few hours. A ladybug's color develops like that of a self-developing camera—in the sunlight. If you find a lightly colored ladybug, you can actually watch it darken right before your eyes.

Who Am I?

My first name means "small." The markings on my back are somewhat scary. They seem to remind some people of the bandits who sailed the seas. You might be able to guess my name if I called you "Matey." **Who am I?**

(Minute pirate bug)

Hopping and Skipping and Spitting

Grasshoppers, like ladybugs, will spit when you pick them up. Being eye to eye with a grasshopper could result in your being covered with their "tobacco juice" spit. Once you've been spit on, you never will forget it. This spitting is how a grasshopper defends itself, and it seems to work quite well.

What do you get when you cross a pig and a centipede?

Bacon and legs!

To set up the area for the contest, get some string or crêpe paper to mark off the measurements of lengths for spitting. Rocks work nicely to hold down the string or crêpe paper. Now, all you need to do is give everyone a slice of watermelon and a spitting order (as you will only want one person spitting at a time). Then, line them up at the starting line and let them spit their seeds one at a time, while someone marks down their score or distance. The winner is the person who spits the farthest. Remember to spit in the spitting area only and not near or on anyone, and the game will remain fun.

Tolerance Tests

If you're not into spitting, you can always try sitting—hold an ice-sitting contest instead. All you need are a few willing contestants, a plastic chair for each one, and some ice. Timing all your participants, see who can stand it (or rather sit on it) the longest. It may sound strange, but a lot of bugs would do very well in this competition. Many insects have an "antifreeze" type of blood in them, so they won't freeze. Other insects adapt to whatever the temperature is around them. Maybe your friends and family will adapt too!

Everyone reacts differently to different things; some people like heights while others can't stand them. Maybe you can tolerate or withstand cold. Maybe your brother likes the heat better. Famous shows and acts spotlight performers who can tolerate heat by walking on coals or swallowing flames. Some insects tolerate living in boiling geysers. Some bugs live in crude oil.

You can try tolerance tests on your friends or family too. Maybe you can see who can walk the farthest over a surface covered with pebbles without wearing shoes. Maybe your challenge will be timing who can hold their breath the longest. And there's always the test of who can eat sour lemons!

Can you eat rhubarb with salt on it? Or a tomato or dill pickle with sugar? How long can you sit with your back against the wall with a pretend chair under you? Can you stare without blinking? Can you survive tickling?

Who Am I?

I could be a kind of bug that is not easily swallowed. You might think you would need to see a doctor to get me, but you can usually find me in dead or decaying plants. I have gills and I like to roll up in a ball. My name rhymes with ill. **Who am I?**

(A pill bug)

Screaming, Crying, and Hissing

If you are threatened, would you try screaming and crying? Or maybe even hissing? It wouldn't be a bad idea. And it certainly works for many bugs. For example, if you catch a long-horned beetle, it's bound to start crying. On the other hand, a bess beetle will squeak or scream when someone picks it up. The voice of a death's head hawk moth sounds hauntingly like a real voice when this little bug blows squeaking sounds through its nose.

Some insects make clicking sounds, whereas others make musical sounds, like the cricket. The sound a cricket makes can lull you to sleep or it can tell you the temperature outside. These little cricket thermometers need only to chirp to tell you the temperature. When you hear a cricket chirping, count how many chirps you hear in fifteen seconds, then add forty to that number. The total of these two numbers should be the temperature in degrees Fahrenheit outside.

You can hear a deathwatch beetle's ticking sound over a great distance. Believe it or not, it makes this ticking noise

by banging its head on a piece of wood. A bumblebee buzzes to let you know it's around, and a hissing cockroach hisses when you pick it up. In the evenings, cicadas make noises that sound like a buzz saw sawing away in nearby trees. Katydids sound like they are saying their own name. And did you know that ants make sounds too? People have reported hearing strange sounds that were eventually traced to the underground colonies of ants.

▶ Try This

Hear the Bug Band Play

Try sitting outside around sunset and listen for the sounds of the insects talking to each other. Now, see if you can locate any of them. Sometimes they will stop talking as you get closer. Think of it like the hot and cold game, where you need to narrow down the location by the sounds until you find the bug that's making the noise.

FUN FACT

Did You Know?

Did you know that itching powder is sometimes made from the ground-up hairs of tarantulas? Gross, huh? Just thinking about it can make you itch!

Silly Self-Defense Skills

What some bugs wouldn't do for self-defense! Springtails spring to escape from their predators. Worker termites vibrate leaves with their abdomens, imitating the sound of a snake to scare off any would-be passerby. Stinkbugs make such a stink that everyone leaves them alone. And the caterpillars that make their home in the beans of a Mexican shrub can make their bean home jump to get away from their predators. Other insects will pretend they're something else, like the death's head hawk moth caterpillar. When threatened, this caterpillar puffs up its thorax until it looks just like a snake.

Arachnophobia

Someone who has arachnophobia has a fear of . . . what? Color in all the triangles to see what kind of scary bug you find!

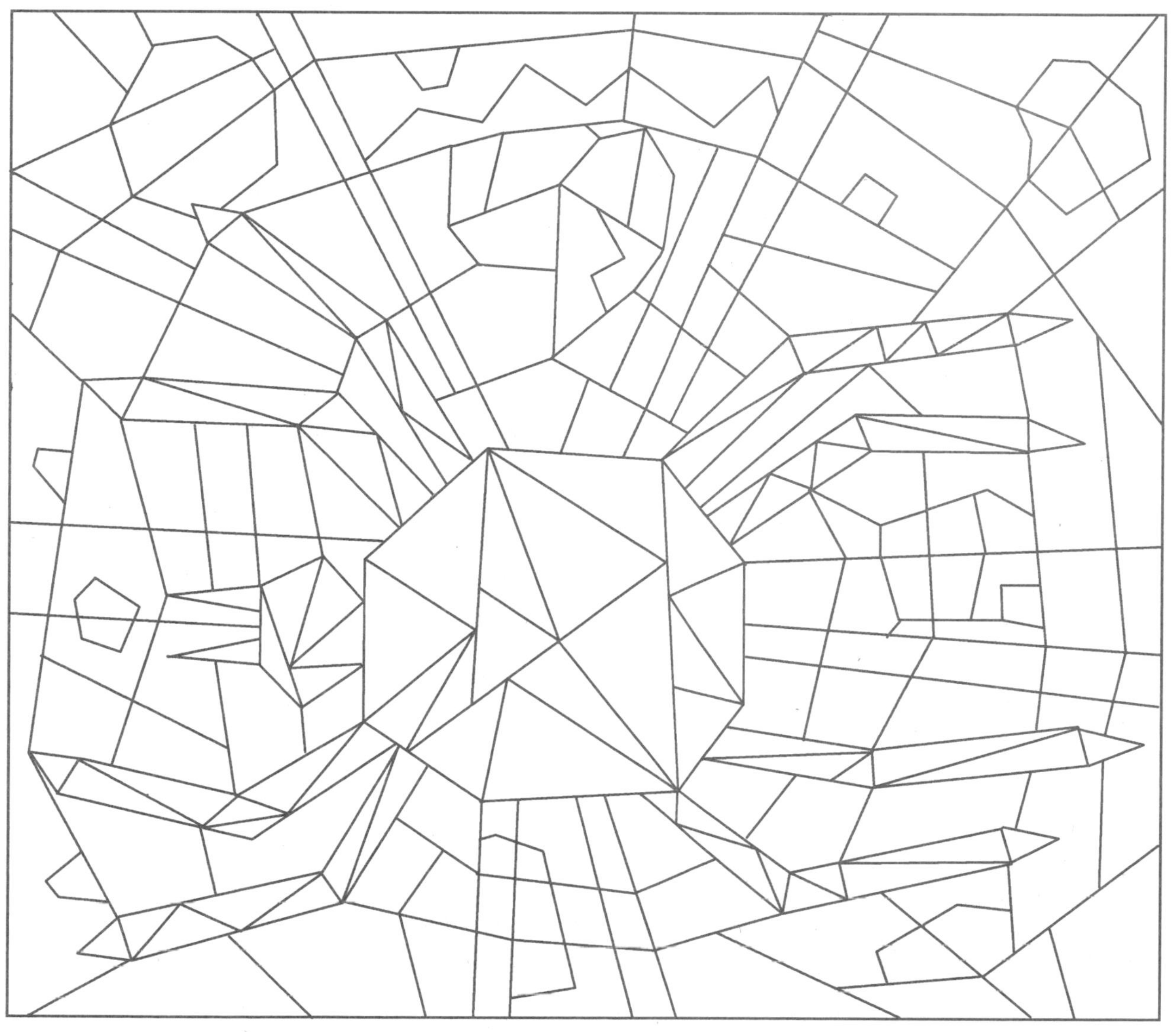

FUN FACT

Funky Feet

Flies hang from the ceiling with the help of little sticky pads on their feet, which allow them to walk up and down walls and upside down. And they also use their feet to taste! Once they have stepped into something good, they soak it up with a spongelike mouth.

Fly Tricks

And, as you know, flies simply fly up to the ceiling, where it's almost impossible to reach them. Don't you wonder what the view is like from up there? Lying with your back on the floor, look up. Now, try to picture your room from a fly's point of view. See if you can draw what you think the fly sees. Is everything upside down?

Flies have compound eyes. (Do you remember what those are? If not, see Chapter 1.) That's why they can see so well, and in all directions—you can never sneak up on a fly. We humans, on the other hand, have a blind spot. How do we know? Well, you can prove it to yourself. All you need is a piece of plain white paper and a pen.

Draw a line about 3 inches long in the center of the paper. On the left end of the line, draw a fly. Don't worry if it's not a very good picture of a fly, as long as it's a small picture. Then, draw a small X at the opposite end of the line. Now close your right eye and leave it closed. While holding the paper in your left hand, look at the X with your left eye. Now, slowly move the paper forward and then back. If you stare at the X the whole time, you should notice that the fly disappears when you reach the right distance from your eye. That's the blind spot. You've probably never noticed it before, because when you use both of your eyes at the same time, one eye takes over for the other, so you don't know that you have a blind spot.

Blind Art

If you're feeling artistic, you could paint something blindfolded. This will work best if you are outside and dressed for the activity. Using a large poster-board, paint with "feeling" or "expression," rather than sight, the way many famous artists

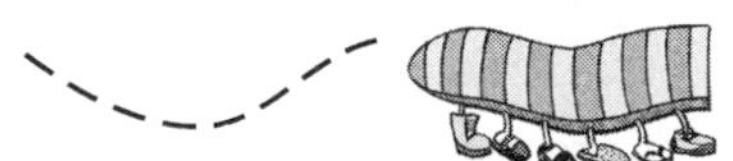

have done over the years. These artists also did splatter painting, painting with other body parts (their feet, for instance), and dot painting. If you look very closely at one of these famous paintings with a magnifying glass, such as *Sunday Afternoon on the Island of La Grande Jatte* by Georges Seurat, you will see that thousands of dots create the larger picture.

What do you call a park that's filled with millions of tiny biting bugs?

A gnat-ural disaster!

▶ Try This

Nose Painting

How about making dot painting, using your noses. To do this challenge, all you'll need is:

- A blindfold
- A soft canvas to paint on
- A damp washcloth for cleaning up
- A plastic lid with different colors of washable paint spread on it
- A friend to guide each "painter" to the painting

Someone will lead the blindfolded painters to the canvas, where they dip their noses into the paint and make their marks on the canvas. Together, you can create a great mural that will make you famous in the world of art and nose painting.

Dangerous Bugs

predator: An insect or any other animal that hunts other animals for food. Here are some examples of predators: Lacewing larvae disguise themselves with the wooly wax they steal from the wooly alder aphids. Once the lacewings are covered in the wool, they sneak in and eat the unsuspecting aphids. Assassin bugs grab the already captured prey in a spider's web for their meals.

Bugging a bug can be downright bogus—and dangerous! Messing with some insects can be deadly. What will an insect do to win a battle with a predator? A dragonfly nymph juts out its jaw of hooks, piercing its opponent, while a puss moth caterpillar whips its tail and spits acid at its attackers.

The black bulldog ant can get really mean. It not only bites, but it also stings its attacker at the same time. And the yellowtail moth can give you a rash just by touching its hairs. The darkling beetle has this trick up its sleeve: It will stand on its head and spray a fluid all over its would-be predator. The sawfly gums its attacker or prey to death. The scorpion strikes those who threaten it with the telson, a spike at the end of its tail.

Earwigs use their horned feelers (antennae at the end of their tails) to protect their eggs and young. Some caterpillars simply poison anyone who touches them with their venom-filled hairs. Aphids kick small wasps that try to bother them. Crickets wrestle and bite their opponents to death. Horsefly larvae drag the tiny toads that come too close down into the mud and suck all of the juices out of their bodies. The bombardier beetle bombs or sprays its attackers with a gas. This gas removes all

Which U.S. president became a butterfly?

Jimmy Carter-pillar!

▶ Try This

Make Your Own Fire Extinguisher

With the help of an adult, you can see just how a fire extinguisher works. Take a small plastic bottle and pour five teaspoons of vinegar inside. Then, light a candle and set it on a plate. Now add a teaspoon of baking soda into the bottle with the vinegar. Gently tip the bottle straight toward the flame, and see what happens.

the oxygen they need from the air, so that they are unable to breath, and stop dead in their tracks. This is how fire extinguishers work too: they provide a rush of gas to get rid of any oxygen, which is what keeps the fire going.

FUN FACT

Voracious Appetites

Some insects will eat almost anything, even dead animals. In fact, these creatures are the cleanup crew of the animal world—and you'd be amazed how quickly they can turn a dead rodent into a pile of bones.

Bug Attack

Here's a fun idea to try to fool your friends and family. Create fake bugs and stick them everywhere. All you need to do is cut out some pictures of real insects and stick them onto clear tape. Once you attach the tape to a surface (like a plastic trashcan, the fridge, the computer screen, or a mirror), it will look as though the insects are real! Any other places where you can leave your bugs? How about on a pillowcase or an apple? When you find a good place, make sure that you do not destroy anything with the tape and that you will be able to pull it off later on.

Insects Who Eat Us!

Okay, it's time to admit the truth. Not all bugs attack in self-defense. Some are just plain hungry. Face it, bugs eat us too. When was the last time a bug bit you? Chiggers, a part of the family of fleas, do it. So do lice. Mosquitoes quench their thirst on human blood and so do ticks, vampire flies, and mites. Do all those pesky mosquitoes have you seeing red? Well, your friends will be seeing red too (blood red, that is), if you serve them "I Scream" Cones.

To make the "I Scream" Cones, take a package of regular flat-bottom ice-cream cones and place them in a muffin tin. Then, mix up a regular cake mix and fill the cones one-third of the way full with the batter. Bake them at the temperature

recommended on the cake-mix box, carefully watching the cones, as they will cook more quickly than the cake will. When the cakes are done, remove them from the oven and let them cool. Fill the cone almost to the top with strawberry pie filling and gummy candy worms or edible candy eyeballs. Before serving them to your "unaware" guests, scoop some ice cream on top and prepare for the screams!

Slurp It Up!

Bugs that prey on animals for blood have a special mouth shaped like a straw, which they use to puncture the skin and slurp up the blood. These straw mouths are very handy. Have you ever tried to drink a milkshake without a straw? You wouldn't get very far, would you? Of course, you can also eat a burger and French fries. Most of these bugs, however, survive on liquid meals. Here's what a fly does, for instance: It spits on food first, then waits for it to dissolve so that it can slurp it up with its straw mouth.

A box of straws can provide hours of fun, if you know how to use them. Play a game of "pick up straws": Dump the contents of the box of straws onto a table and have each contestant pull out one straw from the pile without crashing it. You can keep score by counting the number of straws each person can manage to pull out before the pile collapses.

▶ Try This

Let the Sipping Begin

Try eating some different foods with a straw. Is it working? Maybe you can use two straws as chopsticks? After you get some practice, challenge your friends to an eating race. Something slimy like apple pie filling with a straw sounds fun. How about eating blindfolded (doing this outside would be best)?

Chapter 8

Riding Bulls/ Riding Waves

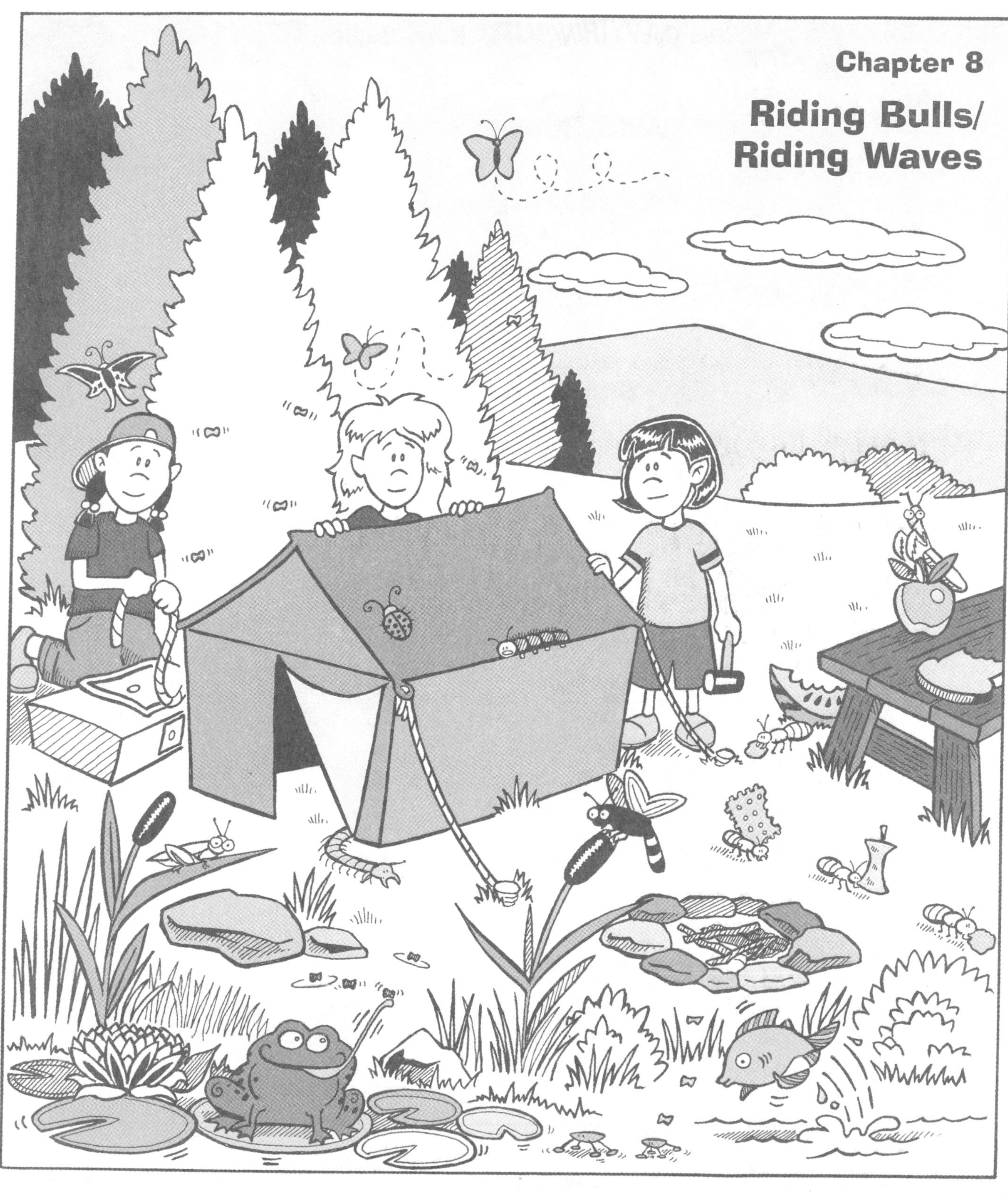

Wild Rodeos

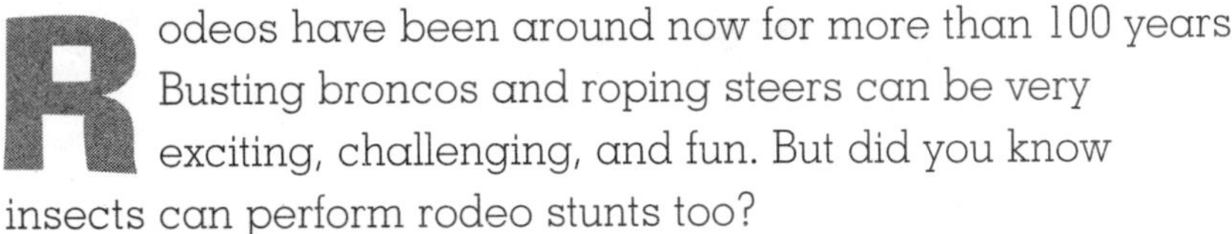

Rodeos have been around now for more than 100 years. Busting broncos and roping steers can be very exciting, challenging, and fun. But did you know insects can perform rodeo stunts too?

You can buck a stag beetle if you gently push down on its abdomen or lower back. The bucking beetle will raise its pincers up in an attempt to reach you. If you repeat this a few times, the stag beetle will flip over as it tries to keep its balance. Fighting stags will turn each other over and try to knock each other off of limbs or rocks to win a battle.

Blister beetles like to ride bareback on bees. And baby water bugs can ride around on their father's back until they hatch without being bucked off. Some of these bugs may shake before takeoff, which makes them look scared, but the reason they shiver is to warm up their bodies before takeoff. Male scarab beetles fight with their horns just like bulls do, and the winning beetle will use its rhinoceros-like horn to throw the loser through the air.

▶ Try This

Play the Pincer Game

You and a friend can challenge each other to a stacking game. Using two pairs of tongs and boxed items like pudding and cake mixes and packages of cookies, you can see who can stack the tallest tower with the tongs in a short period of time—you can ask someone to clock you. For a more difficult challenge, try stacking coins, sugar cubes, or dominos.

Barrels of Fun

Barrel racing is another popular rodeo event. But, how about barrel tracing? To barrel trace you will need a quarter, a pen, a ruler, and a piece of paper. First, use the ruler to draw a straight line across the center of the paper. Place the quarter above the line and trace all the way around it. Next, move the quarter over about ¼ inch to the right and trace around it again; keep moving and tracing the quarter until you have four circles.

Looking at all the circles together, you should see a barrel. Does the left end or the right end of the barrel seem closer to you when you look at it? Turn the page upside down and look at it again. Now which circle or end seems the closest? Is it the same end? Draw several more circle barrels on the same page. Does it look like all the barrels are facing the same way? Try this trick on a friend. What do they see? What happens if you use a different colored marker to trace each of the four rings instead?

Who Am I?

You can find me in the desert where water is scarce. When I'm thirsty, I stand on my head and wait for the wind to blow. Moisture in the air gathers on my legs and back, and slowly drips its way down to my mouth. **Who am I?**

(A darkling beetle)

Water Bugs

Another place to find insects is in the water. You'll see them swimming, skating, and snorkeling in there. Backswimmers float on their backs with a little help from the air-filled hairs that cover their body. As a matter of fact, they float so well, they have to hold on to something to go down under the water. Water skaters skate across the top of the water searching for food. Diving beetles use their wings to store the air they'll need while they are underwater; when they surface, they stick their tails in the air to breathe again.

Many insects breathe through spiracles and air tubes. The spiracles are holes, or openings, in the skin that are attached to the air tubes. Rat-tailed maggots breathe through a telescoping

spiracle: A spiracle is an opening in the exoskeleton of an insect. Through this opening, the air moves into a network of tubes, allowing the insect to breathe.

tail. Similar to a periscope, the tail becomes shorter or longer, allowing the maggot to breathe underwater, whether it's close to the surface or deep underneath. Mayflies use gills rather than air tubes to breathe (just like fish do), because most of a mayfly's life is spent underwater—in fact, it can't survive for more than a day after leaving the water.

The water siphon snorkels in the air it breathes. The water measurer gets its name from pacing off the water in the same way an inchworm measures the ground. Squirting water out of its abdomen sends a rove beetle zipping across a pond or lake.

Practice Siphoning

"Siphoning" is just a fancy term for getting water to move "up" from one container to another through a pipe in the shape of an inverted U. You can practice siphoning with straws. To try it, take two flexible straws, squishing the end of one and inserting it into another, making it into one long straw. Next, you'll need a tall glass of water and an empty dish sitting beside it. Dip one end of the straw into the glass of water and place the other end into your mouth. Suck on the straw, until you start getting some of the water in your mouth. Drop the end from your mouth into the dish. The water should empty from the glass into the dish. If it doesn't, try again. Air bubbles can cause the siphoning to stop, so you may have to pinch your straw while you drop it to the dish.

Do you know the record for the world's longest straw? Maybe you can beat it. How long of a straw can you make with a whole box of straws? Try it and see! Once you have your super-long straw, can you drink out of it? Have a friend help you hold the end of your straw in a glass of water, while you try to drink from the other end.

FUN FACT

"Whirly" Who?

Whirligigs have four eyes, two on top of the head and two underneath. This allows the whirligigs to see everything that is going on above and below the water. Whirligigs, also known as *water beetles*, make good aquarium pets. You'll know one when you see it by the whirling motion it makes on top of the water.

Magic Water Tricks

You can perform several magic tricks with water. One of the simplest ones is to flip a bucket of water upside down without spilling it. Want to know how to do it? Find a bucket or a small pail and fill it three-quarters of the way with water. Holding the handle in your hand, extend your arm out and swing the pail around in a large circle. If you swing fast, you won't spill a drop!

Speaking of magic treats, ever heard of walking through a five-by-seven index card? Sounds impossible, but it's easy. To prepare, take the index card and fold it in half the long way. On the side that is folded, make a cut toward the unfolded side, stopping ¼ inch before you reach the end. Turn the paper over each time and make these cuts one by one, ½ inch apart, always stopping ¼ inch from the end. Then, open the card up and cut all the way down the fold *except* for each end. If all of the cuts are in the right places, your card will open up into a paper circle that you can walk through.

What's smarter than a talking parrot?
A spelling bee!

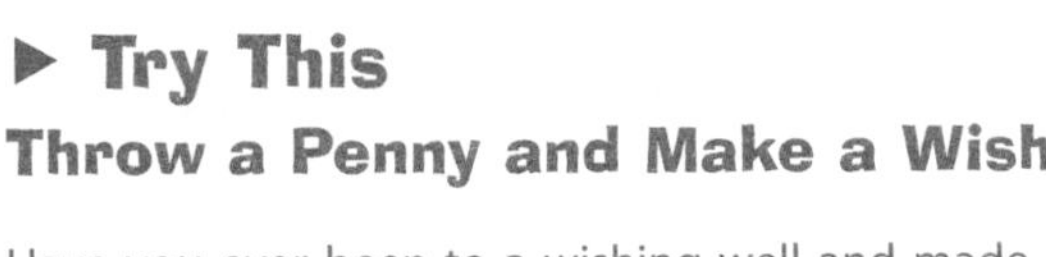

▶ Try This
Throw a Penny and Make a Wish

Have you ever been to a wishing well and made a wish? Traditionally, as you make a wish, you throw a penny into the water to help it make your wish come true. And maybe that is where the water penny got its name. Or maybe someone saw one of these penny impostors in the well, and thought they should throw a penny in too!

Water pennies grow up in the water and don't come up to the surface until they are adults. How can they stay under water for so long? They have gills—and so do the larvae of damselflies, mayflies, and dobsonflies, to name a few.

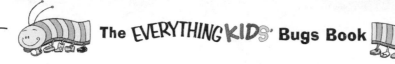

Water Relays

Now it's time for a more energetic activity. How about a water race? To race, you'll need two teams and two small tubs of water to place on their heads. Each team sends a player (who must carry the tub of water on his or her head) to a landmark and back. Both teams race to see which side finishes first. But the tricky part is that you can't rush too much, or you'll spill all the water! The winning team must have some water left in their tub to win.

You can also play a game of water toss. Spread both teams out over a yard, so that teammates are spread out in a line and each player stands next to his or her opponent. Each player should have a plastic pail. The first pair's pails should be filled with water. When the game begins, the first two kids run to their respective teammates and pour the water into their teammates' empty pails, who then in turn run to their other teammates, until the last person on each team receives the water and runs to the finish line. The winner is the fastest team with any water left in the last pail.

Bug Olympics

Every year, Purdue University hosts the Bug Bowl, complete with cockroach-racing competitions. If you think you'll be in Indiana during April, why not stop by to cheer for your favorite bugs?

Making Milkweed Boats

As autumn approaches, you'll see the pods of milkweed plants begin to open. The seeds inside are great for starting that butterfly garden, and the pods make great boats. The canoe-shaped pods, whether they are green or brown, are fairly seaworthy. Try floating a pod in a pan of water or a pool. If it seems to need more weight in the bottom or if you want to add a sail, press a small amount of clay in the center of the pod. Your sails should be fairly small so they won't tip your boat over. A piece of a straw and a sticker or two for the sail should work nicely. Now, it's time to improve upon your design. Will it sail faster with more or less weight in it? Is a bigger boat

Water Slide

Follow this bug called a "pond skater" across the water from START to END.
Remember—don't cross the lily pads!

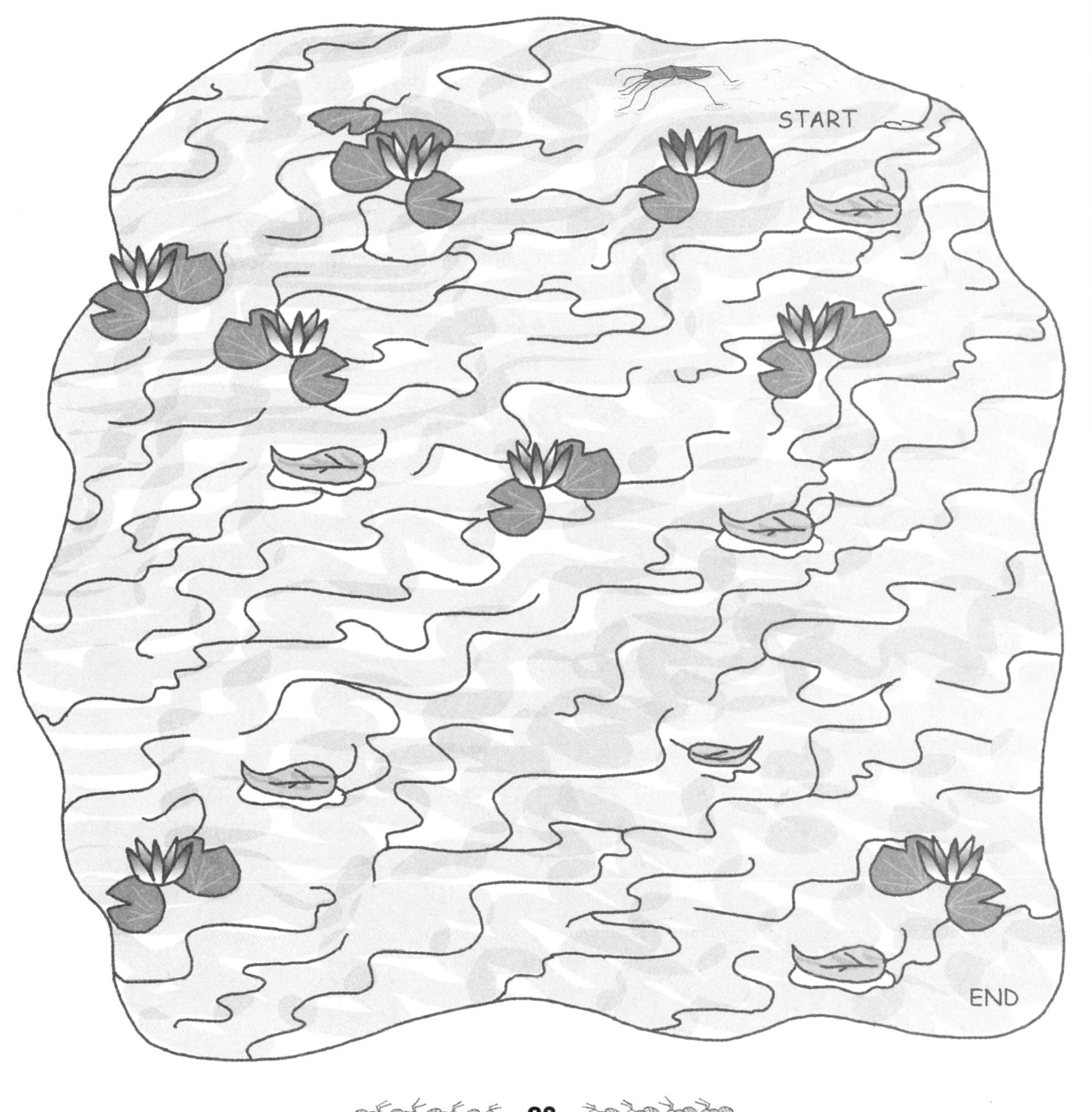

faster or slower? Should you use a V-shaped pod or one that's more rounded?

Once you think you've got the fastest and sleekest boat, you're ready for the competition. You and a friend can test your sailing craft in a real pool or pond. Make sure you take your parents along with you to watch the competition. You may even be able to talk them into having a family picnic and day of milkweed sailing at a nearby lake.

If you go to a place where you can go swimming and the water is shallow, you can conduct a floating/sinking experiment. Gather together some items and then guess whether they would float or sink. After you record your guesses, you can actually test the results by placing the objects you've picked in the water. Here are some objects you might be interested in testing:

- A can of **regular soft drink**
- A can of **diet soft drink**
- A **plastic lid**
- A bottle of **water**
- A **spoon**
- A piece of **wood**
- A **quarter**
- An **orange**
- **Anything else** you want to try

Then, it's time to play Marco Polo. This game is named after a famous thirteenth-century explorer who journeyed from Italy to China along the Silk Road. To play Marco Polo, someone is chosen to be "it." Everyone else scatters out in the water and waits. The person who is "it" is blindfolded. To catch the others, he or she needs to call out "Marco." The others answer with "Polo," allowing the "it" person to use the sense of hearing to catch them. Once someone is tagged, he or she becomes "it" and the game begins again.

What's Fresher Than Water?

Most water insects live in fresh water. Humans need fresh water too. As the world's demand for water grows and our supply becomes scarce, we must find new ways to provide fresh water. Water treatment plants have found ways to change salt water into fresh water through evaporation and collection. This has allowed us to adapt to our changing world.

What do you get when you cross a 100-story building and picnic bugs?

Gi-ants!

Walking on Water

Water striders have the magic ability to slide over the water, moving back and forth, without ever sinking to the bottom. How do they do it? Well, they are managing to stay on the water's top layer, which is something like a think film or a top layer of skin. Sounds weird? Well, don't take my word for it! You can actually see this for yourself.

All you need to do is take a cup of water that is almost full and start adding pennies to it one at a time. Watch the top of the cup. What happens to the water? Now, try adding sugar or salt to a different cup that is almost full of water too. How much can you add before it overflows? Was it more or less than you thought it would be?

▶ Try This

Taste Testing

Take 1 cup of water and add 1 tablespoon of salt to it. Taste the water. Now, cover the water and microwave it for 3 minutes. After letting the water cool, taste the water that gathered on the lid. How does it taste? Do you know what happened?

Pour a little puddle of water on a white plate or dish and sprinkle some pepper on the water. Take your pointer finger and put a tiny drop of dish soap on it. Now, touch the surface of the water on the plate. What happens? Can you solve the mystery?

The world is full of mysteries. Have you ever wondered who sighted the first UFO? Have you ever thought that any of the pictures of aliens sort of look like an insect up close? Why do so many ancient cities look like the homes of termites and ants? The most famous unsolved mysteries are:

Why is the letter "A" like a flower?
Because a "B" comes after it!

- Who built Stonehenge?
- How did the ancient Egyptians construct the pyramids?
- What happened to pilots and ship navigators who have disappeared in the Bermuda Triangle?
- Do people really have supernatural powers like the sixth sense, ESP, and mind-reading abilities?
- Does dowsing, or using a divining rod, really work?

▶ Try This

A Water Adventure

Watercourses are easy to make and are a great way to cool down on a hot day. To make your own watercourse you will need a sprinkler, two buckets (one filled with water, the other empty), an empty milk jug filled with water, a tub of water balloons, and a target. Here is how your watercourse will work:

1. First, you run through the sprinkler or jump over it.
2. Then, you make your way over to the buckets where you have to pour the water from one bucket into the other.
3. Then it's onto the jug, where you dump the contents of the milk jug on your head.
4. Finally, you run over to the water balloons and use them to hit the target before your time is up.

How about trying to solve one of these mysteries yourself? See if you can use a divining rod to locate water underground. First, you need to make your own water-finding rod. Ask your parents to get two metal hangers and snip both of them in the bottom left corners with a pair of wire cutters. Then, they should snip both hangers 2 inches above the bottom right corners. As a result, you should have two long almost L-shaped pieces from each hanger. Now, all you need to do is straighten the L shapes out to 90-degree angles, and you're ready to hunt for hidden water or precious minerals.

Place the shorter ends of each L down in the holes of each of your closed fists. Holding the rods straight out in front of you, walk over to a place you already know has water. This could be a pond or a bridge over a creek. If you hold the wires gently but loosely, they should move together and begin to cross over each other the closer you go to the water. Sounds silly? Well, this process really works! People use dowsing rods every day to locate water lines and large deposits of metal. Do you think insects have a way to locate water? Try placing a bug near two flat lids, one that is dry and one that has water. Will the big go to the water? Watch and see!

Darting Dragonflies

On a warm summer day, dragonflies can be seen skimming over lakes and ponds, looking for food or a place to lay their eggs. Dragonflies were also flitting around over 600 million years ago, with one easy-to-see difference. While the biggest dragonfly today has a wingspan of 8 inches, there were ancient dragonflies with wingspans of up to 25 inches. This made them the largest flying insects ever!

Which dragonfly will eat which mosquitoes?

Chapter 9

Between a Rock and a Bug

Prehistoric Insects

Insects have been around for a very, very long time—for millions of years. When dinosaurs roamed the earth, bugs were already there. We know about the dinosaurs from their fossils, which are the hardened remains of their skeletons that archaeologists dig up from underground. And the same is true for our knowledge of ancient bugs. We find their remains in ancient fossils and amber (hardened tree sap that trapped living insects and forever preserved them). While many kinds of bugs still exist today, there are also many that have become extinct and no longer exist in today's environment.

Looking for Insect Fossils

Maybe you've seen a fossil before. If not, you can look for them in small rock beds or around lakes. If you live near a quarry or rock supply, they may be willing to give you a small box of rocks to study.

You can also make your own bug fossils for someone else to discover. To make fossil clay, you will need the following ingredients:

- 1⅓ cups of **salt**
- 2¼ cups of **flour**
- 2 cups of **cornmeal**
- 2 cups of **water**

extinct: When the last member of a species (one particular kind of creature) dies, the species becomes extinct. Many dinosaurs and insects became extinct millions of years ago for reasons not yet known.

▶ Try This
Amber Bug Suckers

Make your own Amber Bug Suckers. Ask an adult to heat up ½ cup of margarine and 1 cup of sugar in a skillet on a medium-to-high setting. Stir the mixture constantly, until it turns the color of peanut butter. Spoon it over several Popsicle sticks on a greased cookie sheet. Then, add gumdrops to make your bug's face and let them cool.

What has six legs, wings, sucks blood, and wears a suit?

A Mr.-squito!

After stirring the dry ingredients together, begin adding water, a little at a time, until the dough sticks together. Now, you can insert a plastic bug or a coin hidden inside each piece of clay and then leave them out to dry. When the fossils harden, you can use them for a fossil hunt. You could also give prizes to the hunters, when they are through, according to the bug they find. Can you think of any good prizes that would match with a particular bug discovery?

You can also make rocks out of rubber. Here's what you need to do: Ask an adult to help you in the kitchen as you heat 1 cup of whole milk in a pan. As the milk simmers, slowly add 1 or 2 teaspoons of vinegar and keep stirring the mixture until it becomes rubbery. Last of all, rinse the rubber in cool running water and shape it into a rock.

Who Am I?

You may have heard the expression "As snug as a bug in a rug." Well, I started that saying. I love to live in your house and eat your rugs and plush carpets. **Who am I?**

(A carpet beetle)

An Ancient Creature

One of the oldest bugs is the cockroach, which has been around for over 200 million years. Little has changed in the world of the cockroach except its size. The cockroach's ancestors were larger, boasting a long 6 inches in size. The modern-day cockroaches are much smaller.

Bug Print

Can you find the fossil hidden in this letter grid? Use a brown marker or crayon to make a line through each word from the list as you find it in the grid. Words can be up and down or side-to-side.

TRICKY PART: The words can appear more than once, and they can also be backwards! One extra tricky word is on the diagonal, and has a bend in the middle!

WORD LIST: CATERPILLAR, LEG, STRIPE, ANTENNA

A U Z N A Z E I Z K E

N L E R Q P K E I H U

H E A U F I H N A Q E

K Q T N I B Q N O J I

G Z R N T O N R S Q K

R P C I A E I A F O A

H O Q H C S C P D I P

E G E L A T A L E G N

I Q N O T R T H R A E

E G E L E I E L E G N

P E Z O R P R H U N L

K G E L P E P L E G U

N A N H I S I N P Z P

R G E L L T L L E G A

I U I H L R L O I R L

E G E L A I A L E G I

P A L N R P R V I N Q

O N P U L E Z P M Z R

P U I R A L Q Z A L O

What is the secret to the cockroaches' success? One explanation is their excellent sense of hearing. Cockroaches can sense your approach simply by the air moving from your direction, which they sense with the hairs that grow on their tails.

Tracing Your Family History

Everyone has some kind of history of his or her own. With a little detective work, you can investigate your own past and build a family pyramid that illustrates how your family came about. To get all the information, you can conduct an interview with your parents, grandparents, and other relatives. They should be able to supply you with a wealth of information for your family pyramid.

To draw your family pyramid, write your name at the top and draw two lines coming down. At the end of those two lines write the names of your parents. Then, draw two more lines down from each of your parents and write the names of their parents. How far can you go? Do you know the names of your great-grandparents?

To make your pyramid more interesting, you can add pictures of each person next to his or her name. You can also do the same type of tree or pyramid with pictures of each person.

Compare the way your relatives look. Did they change a lot over generations, or do they pretty much all look the same?

Since the Earliest Days

The early ancestors of humans, who lived millions of years ago with the ancient insects, had a lot in common with modern-day men. We don't know much about the early people; what we do know we guess from the objects and drawings that they left behind. You can leave a glimpse of your world for someone to discover years from now in a time capsule.

Think of your capsule as sort of like a treasure hunt in reverse. You hide your time capsule today, and in the future someone else will find it. To make your own time capsule, all you need is a glass or plastic jar with a lid. The hard part will be deciding what to put inside. Whatever you choose must represent you and your world. Here are some possible ideas to start you off with:

- **Natural objects** such as butterfly wings or a honeycomb
- **Coins** that you use to buy candies
- A **drawing** of yourself and of your family

Once you've placed all of the items in the container, you could add a piece of paper with the date, place, and time. Then, seal the jar, label it, and cover it with a plastic bag. Now the capsule is ready to be placed somewhere. You can bury it in your backyard or find another place where you think people will find it one day a long time from now.

Who Am I?

Sometimes I am called a harvestman. That may be due to my sudden appearance around harvest time. My relatives are spiders, and you might say I'm the father of the family. I am best known for my really long legs. **Who am I?**

(Daddy longlegs)

Centipede:
Hey, watch out! You're stepping on my foot!

Ant:
Oh, I'm sorry. Which one?

archaeologist: An archaeologist is a scientist who studies life from the past. Many times an archaeologist must dig up the past by digging down in the earth to uncover the buried history.

What You've Left Behind

Another way to get in touch with your past is to have your family help you make a scrapbook about you! Before you were chasing butterflies and catching fireflies, you were learning to walk and talk. One of your first marks on the world was probably your footprint. See how much you can learn about the different stages you went through.

If you want to make bug footprints, you'll need to pour a little grape juice on a plastic lid to let your bugs walk through. Once they've got the sticky juice on their feet, they can leave footprints on a piece of paper. You may be surprised how differently each bug walks and the type of track it leaves behind.

FUN FACT

Unsolved Mysteries

The construction of the pyramids and the curse of the mummy's tomb remain some of the world's greatest unsolved mysteries. How could anyone build something as large and as perfectly constructed as the pyramids at a time so long ago, without the benefit of modern tools and knowledge? And is there really a curse placed on those who bother the tomb of King Tut.

In the Ancient World of Egypt

Have you ever been in a pickle? It's an expression people use for being in trouble. But did you know that people really were "pickled" in ancient Egypt? This wasn't done so that they could be eaten, of course. It served an entirely different purpose: after death, bodies of those Egyptians who were considered important would be preserved for their life after death. This process, known as "mummification," was not all that different from pickling. The body was soaked in salt water and wrapped in linen. Many centuries later, modern archaeologists found these preserved bodies—which we call mummies—in ancient pyramids and tombs, surrounded by the objects of their time.

Making Bone Preserves

One of the best ways to preserve something is to use salt and vinegar. To see if they really work, you can try this experiment.

On a night when you have chicken for supper, save the chicken bones and see if you can preserve them. Take one washed and dried bone and put it in a plastic jar with 1 tablespoon of salt and 1 cup of water in it, and place a lid on top. In the next container, add 1 cup of white vinegar to a clean bone; seal it with a lid. Now, take two small pieces of old broken concrete, place one in a jar of salt water and the other in a jar of vinegar with their lids on. If you find two dead bugs, add two more jars (one with salt and the other with vinegar) to your experiment.

Let all the jars sit for a few days and then check them. What do you see? Did anything change? Which do you think is a better preserving agent, salt or vinegar?

It's Not Rock Candy!

Many people all over the world eat insects. To them, it is no different than it is for us to eat meat. The Australian Aborigines eat the larvae of moths and beetles. Tarantula eggs are popular in Brazil. And canned caterpillars and fried grasshoppers are available year round in Mexico. Eating insects has slowly become more popular for people in the United States too! Insect farms and restaurants are springing up everywhere. The biggest problem is keeping their product from crawling or jumping away.

But maybe you would rather make your own edible bugs? If so, here are a few things you can try:

I don't know why I'm way over here. I don't smell that bad!
#__

- **Raisin water bugs.** First you soak the raisins in water or a favorite soft drink. Then you watch them change and eat them.
- Another treat you can try is **chocolate-covered caterpillars or chocolate-covered worms.** Set a chocolate bar in a microwaveable dish and microwave it for a few seconds, until it melts. Dip some gummy worms or caterpillars halfway into the melted chocolate. Cool the worms on a buttered tray in the refrigerator, until you are ready to serve them.

You can repeat the same process with stick pretzels to make chocolate-covered walking sticks. While you're at it, why not try some other things dipped in chocolate too? Raisins, potato chips, strawberries, pickles, orange slices, or cheese curls would all work. Sounds disgusting? Many things do, before you try them. Another disgusting thing you can try is adding something really weird to a favorite recipe. How about muffins with a soft drink in the batter instead of the usual water? Or try adding strawberry ice cream to your root beer float. Be creative! You never know, you might invent a new world-famous recipe.

Boy, am I HOT!
#__

FUN FACT

Drastic Measures

Did you know that several people have survived in the wild by eating insects until they were rescued? Although insects may not be as delicious as chocolate cake and ice cream, they do have nutritional value and can keep a person alive for a long time.

Splatters of Fun

If the "I Scream" Cone idea (see page 85) isn't gruesome enough, how about dying a T-shirt with red splatters? All you need to do is load a super squirt gun with liquid clothing dye, hang a new white T-shirt from a tree on a plastic hanger (away

A Bundle of Bugs

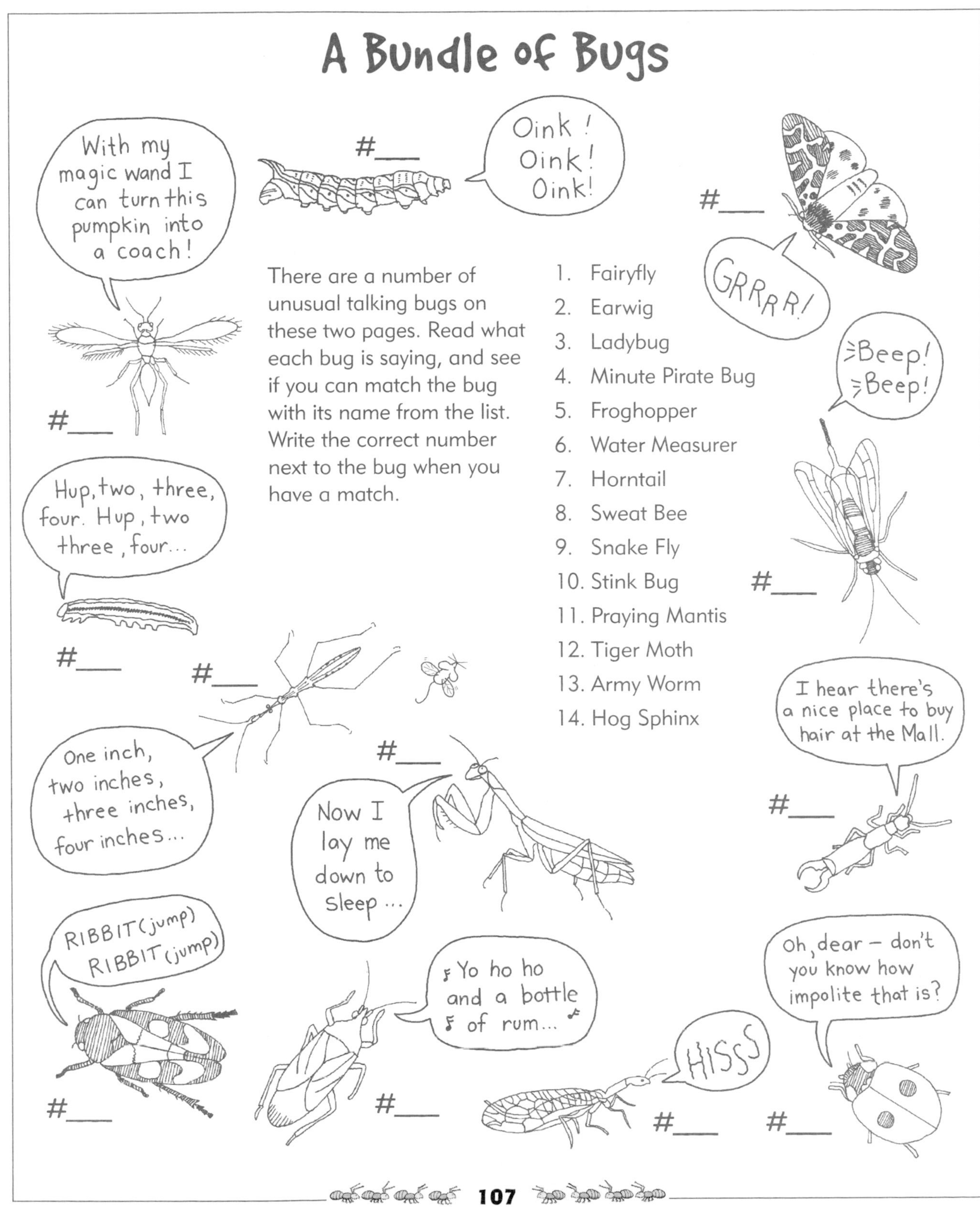

With my magic wand I can turn this pumpkin into a coach!
Oink! Oink! Oink!
GRRRR!
Beep! Beep!
Hup, two, three, four. Hup, two three, four...
One inch, two inches, three inches, four inches...
Now I lay me down to sleep...
I hear there's a nice place to buy hair at the Mall.
RIBBIT (jump) RIBBIT (jump)
Yo ho ho and a bottle of rum...
HISSS
Oh, dear – don't you know how impolite that is?

There are a number of unusual talking bugs on these two pages. Read what each bug is saying, and see if you can match the bug with its name from the list. Write the correct number next to the bug when you have a match.

1. Fairyfly
2. Earwig
3. Ladybug
4. Minute Pirate Bug
5. Froghopper
6. Water Measurer
7. Horntail
8. Sweat Bee
9. Snake Fly
10. Stink Bug
11. Praying Mantis
12. Tiger Moth
13. Army Worm
14. Hog Sphinx

from anything else), aim, and then fire. To get the stain out, your shirt will need to be soaked in cold water in your washer and then washed through a regular cycle of your machine and dried. It is recommended that all dyed items be washed separately to prevent the color from "bleeding" onto other items.

You can also make splatter sunglasses to go with your new T-shirt. Find an old pair of sunglasses and remove the lenses, replacing them with clear cellophane or plastic lenses that you have decorated with marker splatters. How's that for having sunspots in your eyes?

FUN FACT

Bug Medicine

People use bugs for more than just food. In some parts of the world, people let the ants clamp down on their cuts, and then rip their heads off, to hold these strange "stitches" in place.

Bull's Eye

Speaking of spots, how about a game of spotted target practice? To play, you'll need to construct your very own spotted target box. Get a large box or piece of cardboard and draw a target on it with a permanent marker. (A red marker would work best because it's easy to see.) Start with a large circle on the outside. Then, add smaller circles inside each one until you reach the center. Your spots should look like a target.

You may be wondering what you need a target for. It's for your natural "paint" slingshot game. First, you will need to place your target far away from anything you don't want to get messy. Leaning it on a tree would work well. Then, you will need a package of frozen raspberries that are slightly thawed.

You will also need to make a slingshot out of a tree branch that is shaped like a Y. Circle the top of the Y with a rubber band.

Now all you need to do is put a raspberry in the rubber band and pull it back through the center of the Y, and then release it. Your berry should launch itself right into the target. If you need to, you can move a little closer to make hitting the target possible.

What kind of medicine do ants take when they're sick?

Ant-ibiotics!

Ants

Help the ants find their way across the blanket to the picnic. Stop at all the sweet treats, but go past the silverware.

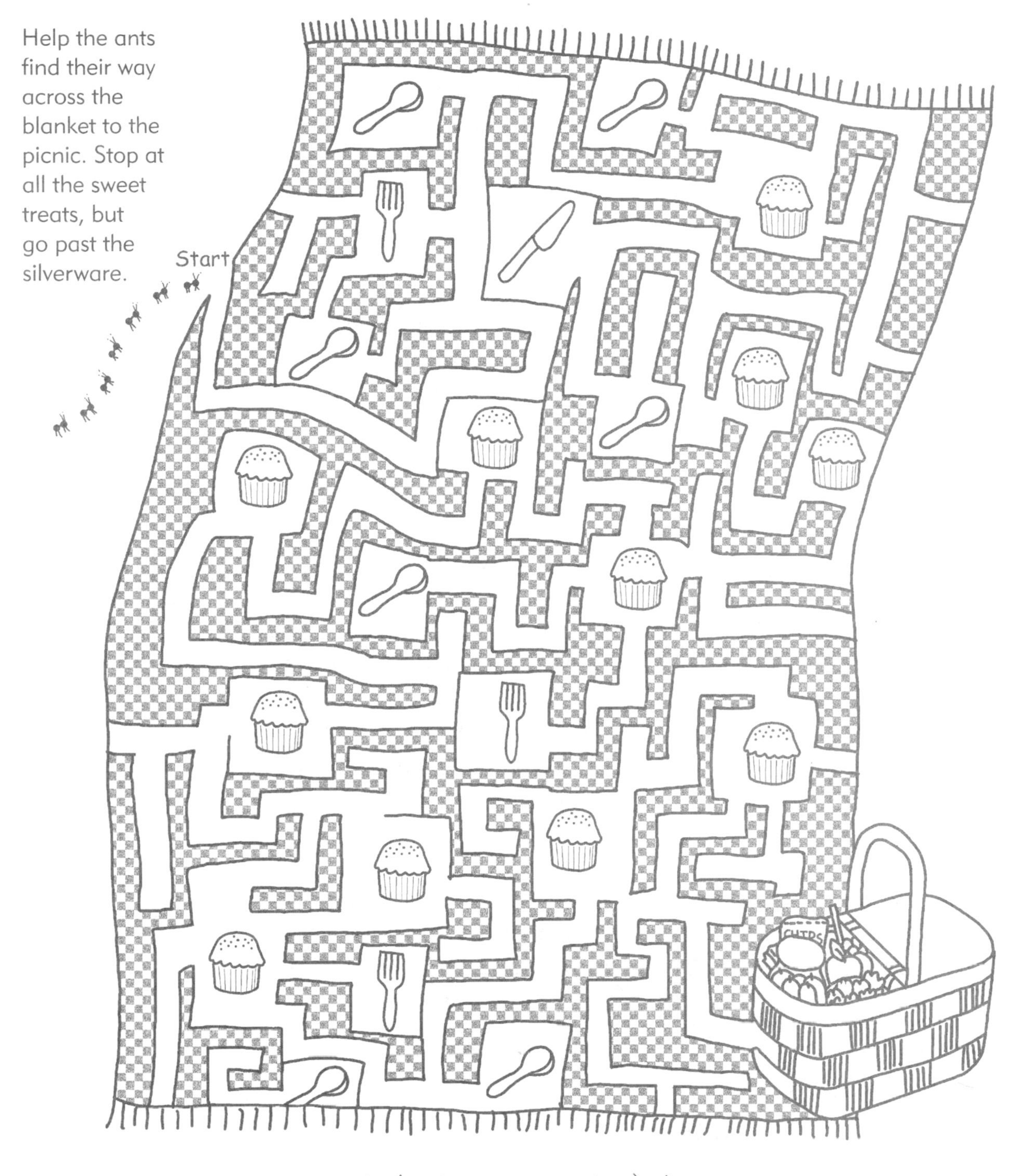

Who Am I?

I am a very rare moth that rises up from out of the ground. When I move my wings to fly, it seems as though I disappear and reappear. Some people have been scared by this haunting effect and that's how I acquired my name. **Who am I?**

(A ghost moth)

How Many Spots Does a Ladybug Have?

Well, that depends. Some ladybugs have only two while others can have up to twenty-eight spots. Each species of ladybugs has a different combination of colors and spots. It's sort of like different breeds of dogs.

Now that you know there are different spots and colors of ladybugs, see how many different types you can spot outside in your yard. If you look at a ladybug up close, you will see that its spotted shell is actually a set of wings, with the second set of wings underneath. These wings are covered with tiny hairs that act like Velcro to lock and hold the wings together when they are being stored.

If you place a ladybug on a stick and hold it up, you will see her walk to the end of it before trying to fly. Watch and you will see it open the first set of wings and expose the second set in preparation for takeoff.

Real ladybugs fly away, but you can keep one for yourself if you make it yourself. How about constructing and decorating a ladybug rock? You can do it in one of two ways:

1. Use a real rock; clean it, wipe it dry, and paint it red, adding black spots and painted-on legs and whiskers.
2. Use fossil clay (see page 100) to make a few round bugs and then let them dry. To decorate them, ask your mom for some red fingernail polish, and make sure you give them enough time to dry.

Chapter 10

Bugs on the Move

Across the United States

The United States is known as the Bread Basket of the World. But we think that it deserves another title as well: the Bug Lunchbox of the World. If you have some of the richest soil and some of the best crops, it's not surprising that you also have some of the hungriest pests on the planet. From California to Connecticut and Alaska to Alabama, guess who's coming to dinner?

It's reported that mosquitoes have been dining on Americans in almost all of the fifty states. Fruit flies are attracted to the fruit of New Jersey. June bugs like the gardens of Minnesota. Bees thrive on the nectar of Pennsylvania flowers.

People have come to America from all over the world; bugs have made a similar transition as well. The Mediterranean meal moth journeyed to the United States all the way from Europe. It made its historic voyage in a few grains of wheat. The earwig sailed across the Atlantic Ocean too—and so did the false belief that earwigs like to live in people's ears! The wood wasp, on the other hand, chose a different destination; it traveled from Europe to Australia.

Some bugs never give up traveling. Tarantulas are famous for stowing away in banana leaves that are exported all over the world. And cockroaches can easily sneak around from place to place. One of their favorite forms of transportation is in the flaps of a cardboard box.

Other bugs hardly travel at all. Take the silkworm moth, for example. This little bug, which produces silk in its caterpillar stage, was one of the best-kept secrets of all time. The only silkworm moths left in existence have been kept in captivity over 4,000 years now for the silk that is harvested from them. For many years, only the Chinese knew the secret of making silk with the help of the silkworms.

FUN FACT

Old Wives' Tales

Superstitions or beliefs about insects have existed for a long time. People used to fear that the sound of the deathwatch beetle was a sign of certain death coming, when the only real death was that of the tree that the beetle was destroying. And some folks still believe that the wooly bear caterpillar's coat of fur can predict whether the upcoming winter will be harsh or mild.

Planning a Trip of Your Own

If you could go anywhere you wanted to, where would you go? Look at a map of the United States—or even the map of the world. What do you know about all those places? Which ones are you interested in and would like to learn more about? Plan out your dream vacation, complete with the places you would like to visit and sights you would like to see. To get more information about traveling, people generally go to a travel agent, who spends all day helping others plan their trips to faraway places. There are also lots of Internet sites where you can get travel information.

If you go on an imaginary trip, why not send your friends an imaginary postcard with an invisible message? It's easy to do. Take a piece of paper and a dish of lemon juice to dip your brush or cotton swab in. Then, write your message with the lemon juice on the white paper and let it dry. To make the message reappear, place the message near a warm light bulb, but not too close—you don't want the paper to catch on fire! The heat from the bulb will turn the lemon juice brown, allowing the message to be read. Other disappearing inks you can use are milk, apple juice, and lemon/lime soda. Try some other liquids you think might work and see what happens!

Why couldn't the butterfly go to the dance?

Because it was a moth ball!

migration: The journey many animals take each year as they move back and forth to avoid difficult climate conditions. The most famous insect migration is that of the monarch butterfly.

When you do go on a trip, whether it's to the next town or to a country halfway across the world, you may be able to find bugs that you've never seen before. You can record what bugs you find and where you find them on a special map or a chart. Even as you move about your own neighborhood, you're bound to see something or someone new. Draw a map of your neighborhood and mark the places where you find any insects. Then, check back on another day. Are they still there or did they decide to travel somewhere else?

Monarch Family Trips

Every year, monarch butterflies go south for the winter. This annual journey, known as a *migration*, is long and difficult. The butterflies cover huge distances, flying from the western part of the United States to southern California and from northeastern states to Mexico.

Butterflies have a very specific schedule. In the spring, they hold courtship rituals, when males and females perform butterfly dances. Then, the female lays eggs, which are soon hatched into caterpillars. As soon as a caterpillar emerges from its shell, it begins eating, and doesn't stop throughout its caterpillar life. The reason caterpillars eat nonstop is because they have to store enough food in them to last them for the rest of their butterfly life. When the caterpillar has reached its full size, it will begin forming its chrysalis, so it can change from a pupa to a full-winged butterfly.

Connecting Caterpillars

How many kids can you hook onto a Processional Caterpillar Line? One kid lies down on the floor and the next one grabs his or her ankles and lies down as well, and so on, until there is a chain of kids holding on to the ankles of the person in front of them. Now that you have your human caterpillar line, it's time to see if you are able to crawl across the floor.

How did you do? You must have noticed that the only way to accomplish this task is through teamwork. Would you be able to walk around if you had as many legs as a caterpillar? To walk, the caterpillar must coordinate the movement of all of its feet. If you look really close at a caterpillar, you'll see that some of the leglike lumps on its body are actually warts or bumps that merely look like feet.

Commuting Moths

Walking is one way to migrate; taking the subway is another. Cotton worm moths are seen quite often hitching a ride on the subways of New York. Springtails hitch a ride on soldier termites and botfly eggs ride on mosquitoes. Red soil mites travel on daddy longlegs and spiders hitch a ride on the wind.

The wind comes in very handy for the butterflies too. They sail it for 100 miles at a time before stopping to rest. Butterflies

▶ Try This
Feeding Butterflies

Butterflies and moths are drawn or attracted to sweet things. If you put a little dab of jam on your finger and sit very still out in the garden, a butterfly just might land on your finger in order to have a snack. The butterfly will unroll its proboscis to drink the jam and then roll it up again when it's through.

migrate in clouds over Africa to the sea. With enough travels, butterflies like the painted lady can now be found in almost every part of the world. Ladybugs also fly to the sea. It seems like a long way for such delicate wings to travel. Buckeyes also migrate each year. If you live on the eastern coast, you might be able to see them traveling up and down the coast along the shores.

Food You Cannot Eat

When you use food items in your experiments, remember that they are off limits to you and your friends! If you feel like snacking on Jell-O, make two batches—one for you and one for your bug visitors.

Leaving Your Mark

If you touch the wing of a real butterfly or moth, you may see what looks like dust on your finger. This isn't really dust—if you examine a butterfly's wing under a microscope, you will see that it is covered by tiny featherlike scales. Each scale holds the pigment or color for the wing. If a butterfly or moth loses too many of these scales, it will be unable to fly.

You can tell butterflies apart by the unique patterns of their wings. What about humans? Is there a way to tell us apart? Well, there is. Each person has a unique fingerprint pattern—no two fingerprints are the same, not even two of your own. That is why investigators dust a crime scene for fingerprints. If they find a print, chances are they may be able to identify the finger (and therefore the person!) it belongs to.

What time is it when a dog starts scratching?

Flea o'clock!

You can make your own fingerprints by placing your fingers in an inkpad and then pressing them over paper. You can also hunt for fingerprints—all you need is some fine powder and Scotch tape. Find a smooth surface where you think you might find a fingerprint (like a glass that someone has drank from), and sprinkle a little fine powder over it. Gently blow any extra powder off, and stick a piece of clear tape on the glass. When you lift off the tape, look for a print (it should be on the tape).

If you want to catch bug prints, buy a box of gelatin and follow the preparation directions on the box; when the mixture is ready, pour it into a small container with a lid to cool until it sets. Then, leave the container out in the open for a fly or another bug to discover it. Check the container for prints and other signs of a bug's visit. If you leave it out for a few days, you may see bacteria begin to grow in the footsteps. Many insects carry bacteria from place to place as they move around.

You may not be able to tell from the footprints, but some bugs walk three legs at a time. Does that sound kind of tough to do? Try it yourself. You can hold a three-legged race by using an old pillowcase or sack to hold your and a friend's legs together and race against other three-legged teams. Or you can hold a six-legged race by having two three-legged teams lock arms together and try to move about.

Who Am I?

You may think that I am the one who came along and frightened Little Miss Muffet away. But it isn't true. It wasn't me. It was actually a wasp. They changed the whole story and added my name just because they needed a bug that would rhyme with "beside her." **Who am I?**

(A spider)

Folding and Unfolding

Butterflies and moths fold and unfold their wings to fly and to rest. If you fold a piece of paper in half, it will look like a pair of wings. How many times do you think you can keep folding the same piece of paper in half again and again until you can't anymore? What made you stop folding? Did you run out of paper?

Something else you can do with a folded piece of paper is to squish or splat a little paint in it. First, fold your paper in half. Then reopen it. Pour a small amount of paint in the middle and fold it back together again. Press the folded paper flat to spread the paint around and then open it. The pattern you see is called an inkblot.

The first inkblots were part of an experiment or test called the Rorschach Test, which was used to see how the mind works. These inkblots and the images we see in them help others to understand what it is that we are thinking. The blots tell a story about how we are feeling. Make up your own story using an inkblot. What do you think has caused you to see what you see in the inkblot?

Mobile Bugs and Bug Mobiles

Bugs have been mobile for many years now, but how do they know where to travel? Do insects have a built-in compass? Some experts believe they do. That would explain why ants always build their nests on the south side of a tree. Or how a termite knows to build its nest with the wide sides facing east and west and the more narrow sides facing north and south. And this approach has a purpose: That way the nest doesn't bake too long in the sun.

Should you ever lose your way out in the forest or desert, take your cue from the insects. You can also get directions from trees. If you live in the northern hemisphere of the world, trees naturally grow and lean to the south as they reach to the sun. If you live in the southern hemisphere, they will grow toward the north or the equator, where the sun is the closest.

But maybe you would feel better if you had your own compass, just to be sure. To make a compass, what you need is a dish of water, a needle, a magnet, and a small piece of paper. First, take the needle and stroke it along one end of the magnet thirty to forty times, so that the needle is magnetized (or charged with magnetic power). Place the small piece of paper on top of the water and then lay the needle on the paper. The needle will slowly move around until it points toward the true north—the North Pole.

Make a Bug Mobile

Bug mobiles can be made out of everyday things like wire hangers and socks. First, you will need to make the bugs that will hang from the mobile. To make a funky caterpillar, wrap a pencil in paper or cloths and then stuff it in your sock. Then, tie the number of sections you want your caterpillar to have on it with pieces of yarn (every 2 inches or so). You can turn this caterpillar into a butterfly if you add cellophane or hose-covered wire wings. Fancy butterflies and caterpillars can be made from white pantyhose or tights.

Add interest with colored tights, or tie-dye your hose before making the bodies or wings. Floral and gift shops carry pearlized cellophane, which looks a lot like real wings. You can add glitter and jewels as butterfly decoration.

When you are done, hang up your creations from the ceiling to form a mobile. A hanger shaped into a circle works well with the bugs all tied on it. Tissue paper cut and folded like a fan works for the wings in a clothespin butterfly. You will want to use the older, round-headed clothespins that don't have a spring in them. When you have the tissue folded, slide it up into the clothespin between the "tongs" of the pin. The tissue should be equal on both sides of the pin. Spread the tissue apart, and tie a piece of elastic thread on the end. You can also dust your butterfly's wings with glitter for a more magical look.

FUN FACT

Microscopic Mites

The smallest moth known is the nepticulid moth, which is about the size of a pinhead. Many insects are so small we can't even see them with the naked eye. Dust mites invade almost every inch of our world, and we can't even see them.

▶ Try This
See the Unseen

To see the almost invisible dust and bugs that are all around you, close your curtains or shades, and turn off all the lights in your room. Now, open the shades or curtains just enough to let a beam of light in. Take a pillow and pat it in the beam of light. What do you see?

X-Country Bugs

These bugs are ready to travel! See if you can match the bugs from the suitcase to the list of clues, then fill the names into the numbered grid. We've filled in one bug to get you started.

HINT: The end of each bug name will rhyme with the city or state name in the clue!

ACROSS
1 Really big spider in Florida
3 Buzzer and biter in Idaho
4 Night-light in New York
5 Field-chirper in Connecticut
7 Branchlike in Phoenix
10 Web-spinner in Montpelier
11 Two-handed bug-grabber in Kansas
13 Spud-eater in Seattle
15 Wood-chewer in Detroit
16 Colorful wings in Kauai

DOWN
2 BONUS: Where's the worst place in the world to have a picnic?
4 Dog-biter in D.C.
6 Almost a butterfly in New Hampshire
8 Nice spotted beetle in Pittsburgh
9 Plant-sucker in Madrid
12 Kind of butterfly in Bismark
14 Honey-maker in Tennessee

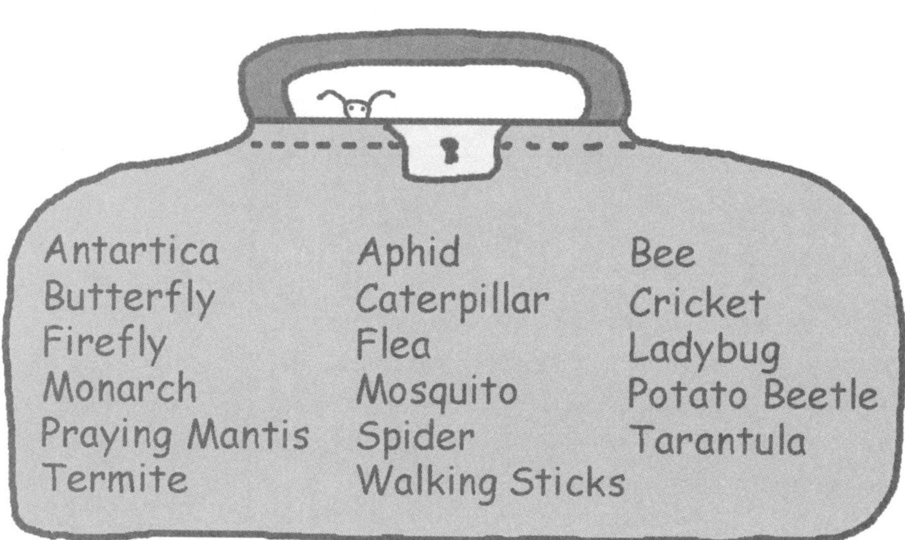

Antartica
Butterfly
Firefly
Monarch
Praying Mantis
Termite
Aphid
Caterpillar
Flea
Mosquito
Spider
Walking Sticks
Bee
Cricket
Ladybug
Potato Beetle
Tarantula

MOSQUITO

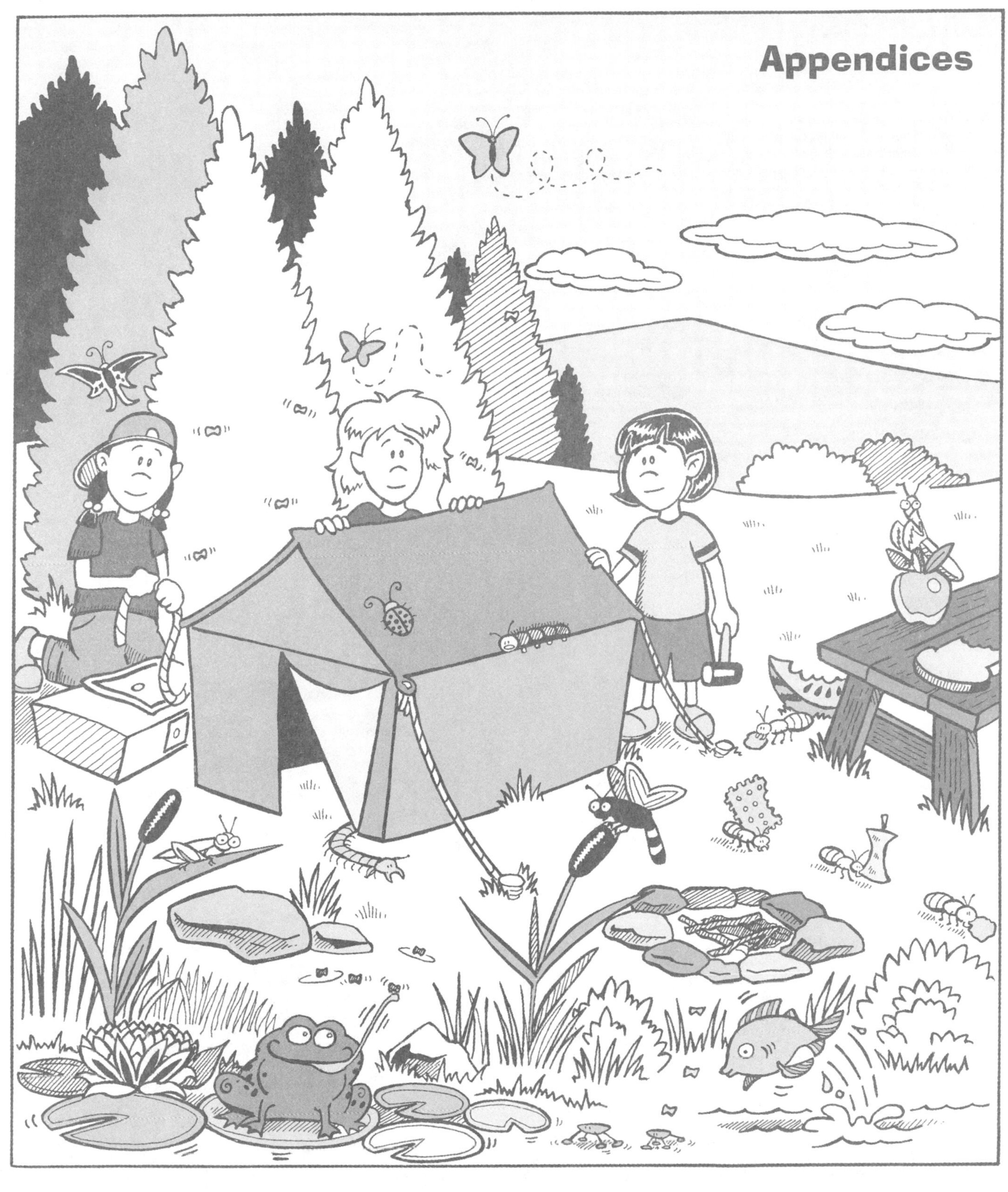
Appendices

Appendix A: Glossary

anthropod: A joint-legged creature. All insects are anthropods, but not all anthropods are insects. Some are just close relatives, like the spider and the centipede. One way to know whether something is an insect is to remember that insects have six legs when they are fully grown.

archaeologist: An archaeologist is a scientist who studies life from the past. Many times an archaeologist must dig up the past by digging down in the earth to uncover the buried history.

breeding: When two insects mate for the purpose of reproduction (producing offspring). Breeding can bring change as two different parents create a new type of baby bug.

colony: In the world of bugs, this is a group of animals or insects (like ants, for instance) that live and work together.

communication: One way an animal or insect gives a message to another. Ants communicate, or "talk," by touching their antennae. Through this touch, an ant can tell the rest of the colony where the food is.

compound eye: Many insects and some crustaceans have compound eyes. Regular eyes receive one big image; compound eyes receive many little images and then put them together into one complete picture. Although an insect's eye may not focus well from a great distance, its vision is excellent up close.

entomologist: A scientist who studies the world and behaviors of insects and classifies them into groups.

extinct: When the last member of a species (one particular kind of creature) dies, the species becomes extinct. Many dinosaurs and insects became extinct millions of years ago for reasons not yet known.

grub: The larvae of some insects before they are fully grown. Many grubs have a wormlike shape to them.

humane: To be humane means to treat other people and other living creatures with mercy and compassion. The word "humane" comes from "human," because this kind behavior is what makes us human. Remember that when you go out on your next bug hunt!

insecticide: A substance created to kill insects or insect pests. Insecticides come in small containers for home use or can be applied by professional exterminators.

marathon: A long-distance race that requires runners to complete 26.2 miles. Although some runners run for speed, for many others the real challenge is in finishing the race. Marathons date all the way back to ancient Greece, when a messenger from the town of Marathon had to run for 26.2 miles in order to carry news of a military victory to Athens.

migration: The journey many animals take each year as they move back and forth to avoid difficult climate conditions. The most famous insect migration is that of the monarch butterfly.

mutate: To change form. Over time, many insect species have mutated into new kinds of bugs. To adapt to an ever-changing planet, certain bugs have learned to eat everything from fabrics to pepper. Many have slowly adapted to temperatures ranging from freezing to burning hot—120 degrees Fahrenheit, to be exact.

predator: An insect or any other animal that hunts other animals for food. Here are some examples of predators: Lacewing larvae disguise themselves with the wooly wax they steal from the wooly alder aphids. Once the lacewings are covered in the wool, they sneak in and eat the unsuspecting aphids. Assassin bugs grab the already captured prey in a spider's web for their meals.

resistant crops: Crops that can withstand or repel disease or pests (such as insects). Crops may be treated with chemicals or have their genetic makeup altered to provide different kinds of resistance.

ringmaster: A person who introduces and is in charge of the acts in the rings of a circus. This person usually wears a top hat and a tuxedo with tails. At almost every single circus performance, the ringmaster will begin with a dramatic welcome: "Ladieeeessss and Gentlemen . . . Welcome to the greatest (or smallest) show on earth!"

self-defense: An animal's way of protecting itself from harm. For example, a wasp will sting not to attack prey, but to protect itself—in self-defense.

spiracle: A spiracle is an opening in the exoskeleton of an insect. Through this opening, the air moves into a network of tubes, allowing the insect to breathe.

Appendix B: Read All about Them!

Boring, Mel and Linda Garrow (illustrator). *Caterpillars, Bugs and Butterflies (Take Along Guide)*. Northwood Press, 1999.

Clarke, Penny and Carolyn Scrace (illustrator). *Insects & Spiders (Worldwise)*. Franklin Watts Inc., 1997.

Haslam, Andrew, et al. *Insects (Make-It-Work)*. Publisher unknown, 2000.

Hines, Marcia. *Killer Bees (Dangerous Creatures)*. Capstone Press, 1998.

Kite, L. Patricia. *Insect Facts and Folklore*. Millbrook Press, 2001.

Klutz (editor). *Spotter's Guide to the Nastiest Bugs in the Backyard*. Klutz, Inc., 2000.

Lovett, Sarah, et al. *Extremely Weird Insects (Extremely Weird)*. John Muir Publications, 1992.

Morgan, Sally. *Butterflies and Moths (Looking at Minibeasts)*. Thameside Press, 2000.

Mound, Laurence and Neil Fletcher (photographer). *Eyewitness: Insect (Eyewitness Books)*. DK Publishing, 2000.

O'Neill, Amanda. *Insects and Bugs (Curious Kids Guides)*. Houghton Mifflin, 2002.

O'Toole, Christopher (Editor). *Firefly Encyclopedia of Insects and Spiders*. Firefly Books, 2002

Pipe, Jim. Taylor, Myke. *The Giant Book of Bugs: And Creepy Crawlies* Millbrook Press, 1998

Ross, Kathy. Holm, Sharon Lane (Illustrator). Crafts for Kids Who Are Wild About Insects (Crafts for Kids Who Are Wild About) Millbrook Press, 1997

Sabuda, Robert and Matthew Reinhart. *Young Naturalist Pop-up Handbook: Butterflies*. Hyperion Press, 2001.

Savage, Stephen. *Insects (What's the Difference?)*. Raintree/Steck Vaughn, 2000.

Wootton, Anthony, et al. *Insects Sticker Book (Spotter's Guide Sticker Books Series)*. E D C Publications, 1997.

Zakowski, Connie. *Insects on Display: A Guide to Mounting and Displaying Insects*. Rainbow Book, Inc., 2000.

Zim, Herbert Spencer, et al. Insects: *A Guide to Familiar American Insects (Golden Guide)*. St. Martin's Press, 2001.

Appendix C: Bugs Online

Ant Farms

24 Hours 7 Days is a company that offers several types of ant farms and kits for any ant farmer. To make a purchase, visit: *www.24 hours7days.com/Bugs/Ant_Farms.html*

Ants, Ants, and More Ants

This is a site for supplies, projects and of course ants! *www.infowest.com/life/ antsants.htm*

BrainPOP

This fun-filled site is crawling with bugs and features activities, quizzes, and Flash videos. Visit BrainPOP at *www.brainpop.com/sci-ence/ plantsandanimals/insects/index.weml*

BugBios

This Web site, at *www.insects.org*, is packed with information about insects, their habitats, and how they interact with humans

Bug Club Home Page

Sign up for the Bug Club newsletter, print out insect care sheets, and join The Bug Hunt at *www.ex.ac.uk/bugclub*

Bugsfood: Insect-Themed Food

When you're ready to cook, visit this site to download fun recipes for food that looks as though it has real bugs in it. *www.uky.edu/Agriculture/Entomology/yth-facts/ bugfood/bugfood1.htm*

DLTK Crafts for Kids

This is a personal Web site that offers puzzles, games, word searches, and arts and crafts ideas—and an entire section devoted to bugs and insects that you can visit at *www.dltk-kids.com/crafts/insects*

Edible Insects

Visit *www.eatbug.com* to get tons of information on raising and cooking insects.

EEK! Critter Corner

This site offers information about butterflies, lightning bugs, dragonflies, and other insects. Visit the Critter Corner at *www.dnr. state. wi.us/org/caer/ce/eek/critter/insect/index.htm*

eNature.com

This field guide to insects and spiders includes facts, insect shapes, and photographs. *www.enature.com/guides/ select_Insects_and_Spiders.asp*

Images of Insects and Their Relatives

This site, maintained by Colorado State University, can help you identify all types of insects with the help of lots of bug pictures. *www.colostate.edu/Depts/Entomology/im ages/images.html*

Insect Scramble

This Nature site lets you unscramble the tiles to reveal the hidden bug. *www.pbs.org/ wnet/nature/alienempire/ multimedia/war.html*

Minibeast World of Insects and Spiders

Quizzes, trivia, games, and insect care information are all found here: *www.members.aol.com/YESedu/welcome.html*

Quia—Insects and Spiders

This site offers online concentration, word search games, and flash cards. *www.quia.com/jg/65608.html*

Tasty Insect Recipes

This site is filled with recipes for making such tasty treats as your own bug blox and banana worm bread. Nutrition information and an insect-purchasing guide are also enclosed. To get cooking, visit *www.ent.iastate.edu/misc/insectsasfood.html*

The Bug Jester

This is a great site for bug jokes, poems, and stories—check it out at: *www.members. aol.com/YESedu/jester.html*

The Wonderful World of Insects

This contains lots of insect information, records, and facts. Plus, visitors get an opportunity to ask a Bug Expert questions about insects. *www.earthlife.net/insects/six.html*

World of Insects

This site can help you find information about insect life cycles and body parts. *www.stemnet.nf.ca/insect*

3D Insects

Learn how to make your own three-dimensional insects at *www.ento.vt.edu/~sharov/3d/3dinsect.html*

PUZZLE ANSWERS

page 6 • **The New Bug in Town**

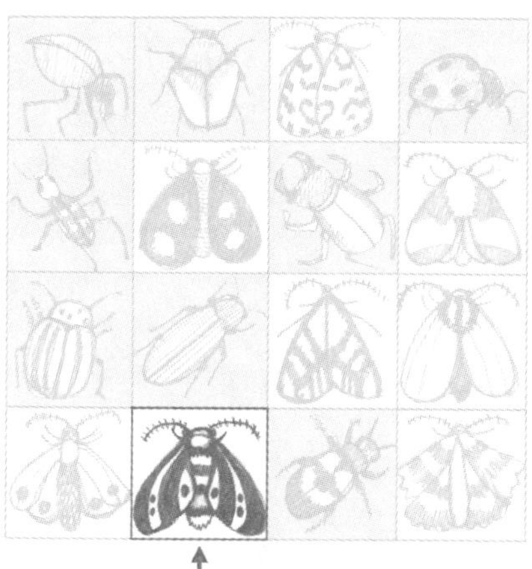

This is the new moth.

page 9 • **Word Caterpillar**

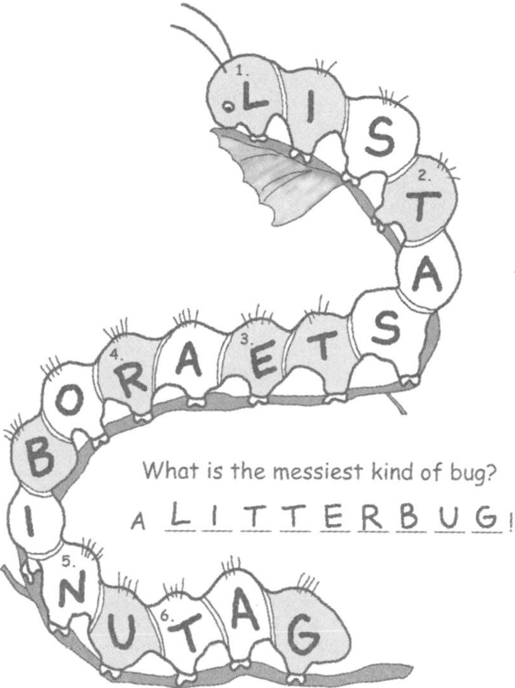

1. L I S
2. T A S
3. T E
4. A R O B
5. I N
6. U T A G
What is the messiest kind of bug?
A LITTERBUG!

page 12 • **Hiding in a Honeycomb**

ant, bee, beetle, fly, flea, ladybug

page 17 • **What's the Difference**

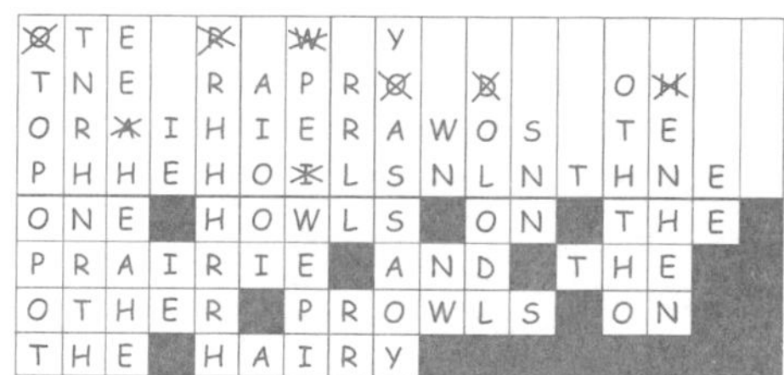

What's the difference between a coyote and a flea?
ONE HOWLS ON THE PRAIRIE AND THE OTHER PROWLS ON THE HAIRY

page 21 • **Smart Bugs Code**

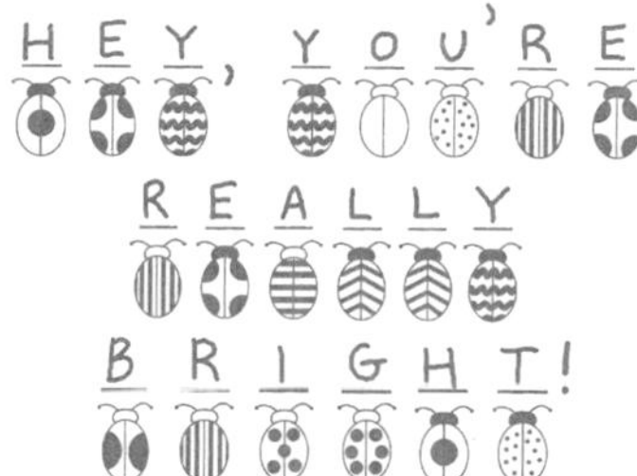

What do you say to a firefly when he gets 100% on his math test?
HEY, YOU'RE REALLY BRIGHT!

page 26 • **Busy as a Bee**

START
END

page 28 • **Mind Your Own Beeswax**

1. handcream 2. lipstick 3. candles

PUZZLE ANSWERS

page 31 • Metamorphosis

START

butter	dish	towel	bar	bell
fly	wheel	chair	man	hole
paper	clip	bottom	less	on
back	door	bell	knob	top
fire	fly	trap	door	secret

END

Words and phrases (in order): butterfly, fly paper, paperback, back door, doorbell, bell-bottom, bottomless, lesson, on top, top secret.

page 41 • Good Bug, Bad Bug

page 35 • Hidden Beauty

Believe it or not, there are many more words that can be made from the letters in metamorphosis! What was the longest word you found?

atom, ear, eat, harp, haste, hate, heart, hiss, hoarse, home, horse, hose, host, mat, mate, meat, met, miss, moat, moose, moss, most, oar, ore, past, paste, pet, photo, pit, poet, poor, port, post, rat, rate, roam, room, roost, root, rose, rot, same, sat, seam, seat, shape, ship, shoot, shop, shore, short, shot, sip, soap, soar, soot, sore, sort, spit, tame, tap, tar, team, tear

page 45 • Hole-y Sweater!

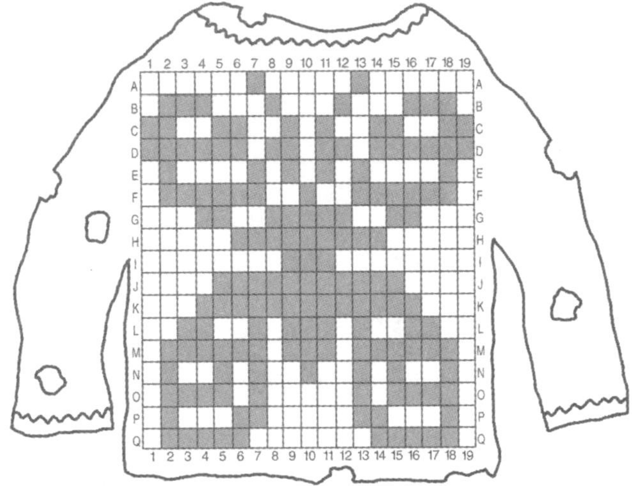

page 36 • Tunneling with Mole Crickets

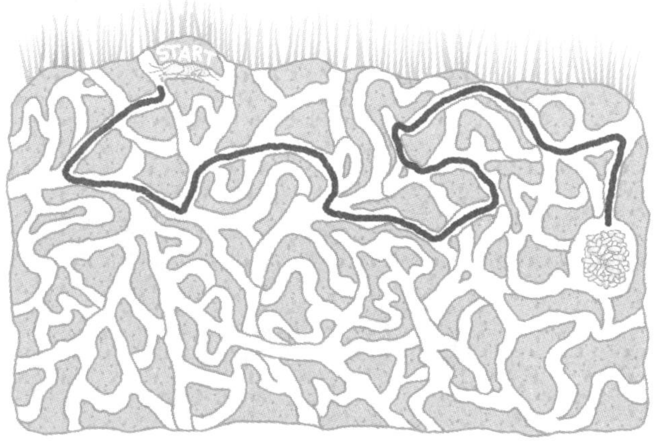

page 53 • Crawly Clues

1. Cinderella's carriage COACH COCKROACH
2. Colorful subject in school ART TARANTULA
3. Tasty dessert PIE SPIDER
4. Type of medicine PILL CATERPILLAR
5. Things worn on fingers RINGS PRAYING MANTIS
6. Red vegetable BEET BEETLE
7. Between shoulder and hand ARM EARTHWORM
8. Move your hand back and forth RUB GRUB
9. Grain served steamed or boiled RICE CRICKET
10. Place to buy things SHOP GRASSHOPPER
11. Man's neckwear TIE TERMITE
12. Vegetable on a cob CORN SCORPION
13. Sturdy work boat TUG STINK BUG

PUZZLE ANSWERS

page 55 • **Bug's Eye View**

1. Looking out of a soda can
2. Grain of salt
3. Edge of a dime
4. Head of a pin
5. Edge of a pencil
6. Hair on your arm

page 60 • **The Ants Go Marching One by One**

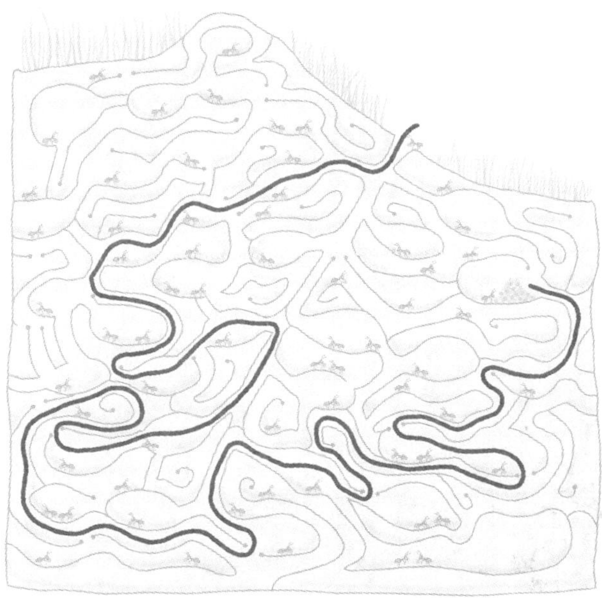

page 64 • **Where's the Bug?**

1. My mother bakes the best cookies.
2. It was Peter's idea to play cards.
3. James was a giant peach for Halloween.
4. Why is a cap hidden under the bed?
5. There's always one beet left over!
6. I need a long rubber band.
7. I'll have a waffle after I finish my juice.

page 68 • **Mixed-Up Flies**

page 69 • **Look-alikes**

Butterfly number 3 is an exact match.

page 70 • **Itsy Bitsy**

A spider walking on a mirror!

page 81 • **Arachnophobia**

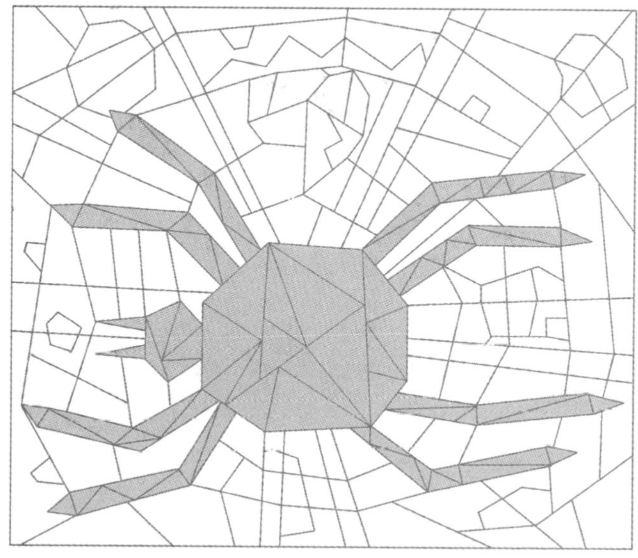

PUZZLE ANSWERS

page 93 • **Water Slide**

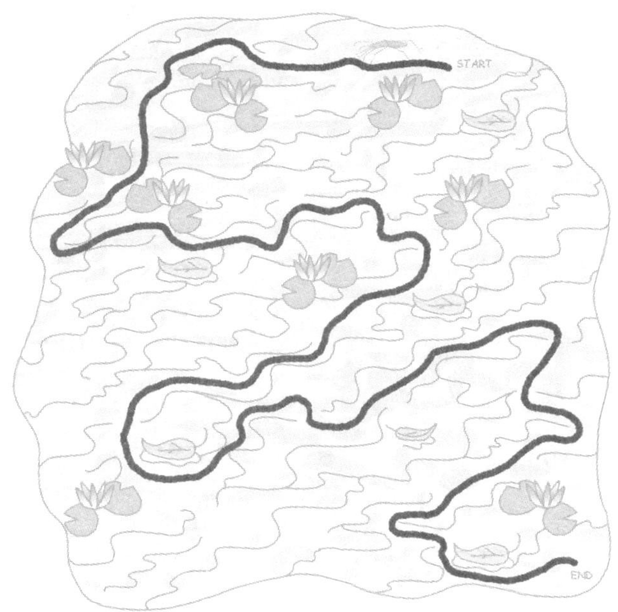

page 98 • **Darting Dragonflies**

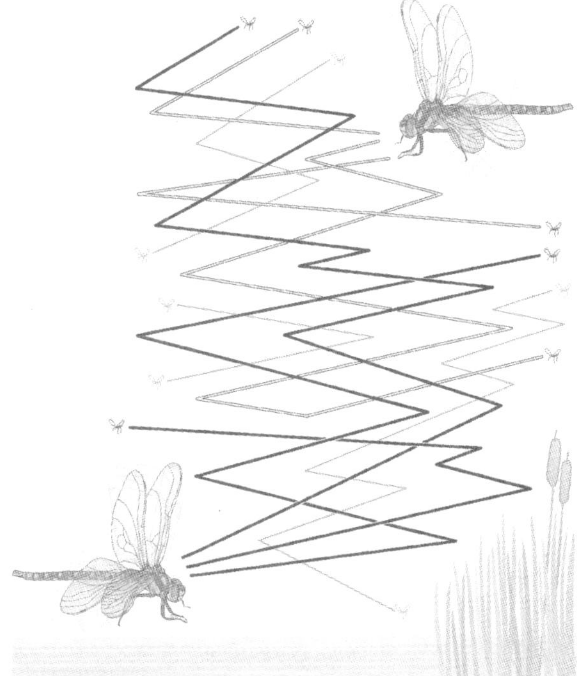

page 102 • **Bug Print**

page 107 • **A Bundle of Bugs**

PUZZLE ANSWERS

page 109 • **Ants**

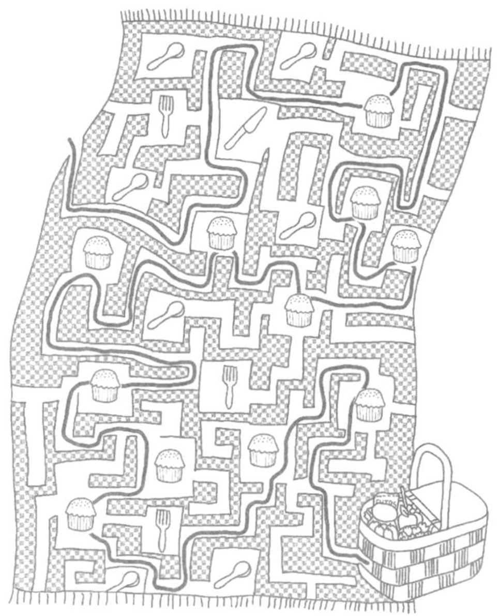

page 120 • **X-Country Bugs**

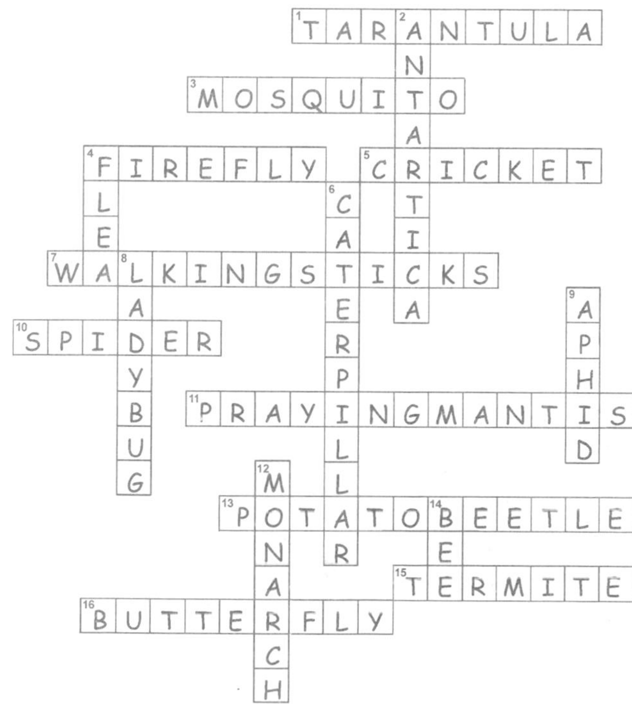

The Everything® Kids' Baseball Book, 2nd Ed.
1-58062-688-2

The Everything® Kids' Cookbook
1-58062-658-0

The Everything® Kids' Joke Book
1-58062-686-6

The Everything® Kids' Monsters Book
1-58062-657-2

The Everything® Kids' Mazes Book
1-58062-558-4

The Everything® Kids' Money Book
1-58062-685-8

The Everything® Kids' Nature Book
1-58062-684-X

The Everything® Kids' Puzzle Book
1-58062-687-4

The Everything® Kids' Science Experiments Book
1-58062-557-6

The Everything® Kids' Soccer Book
1-58062-642-4

The Everything® Kids' Travel Activity Book
1-58062-641-6

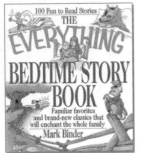

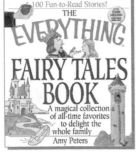